WHAT?
WHEN?
WHY?

by
James R. Webber

PROPHECY POWER

JAMES WEBBER

ISRAEL

Is The Connection To Destruction.

WHAT?
WHEN?
WHY?

A New Perspective On Biblical Eschatology

Prophecy Power
© 2012 James R. Webber
All rights reserved.

All Scripture quotations are taken from the
New American Standard Bible.

By
James R. Webber
Las Vegas, Nevada 89113
USA

Printed in the United States of America

For further information:
jwww@earthlink.net

Cover design by Lacy M. Griner

DEDICATION

To my wife Toni who makes music to the Lord for the Saints. To my son Greg, who is a gift from God. To my son Bart, who is an upright man and who has been on the front lines for Jesus and his wife Kimberly Dawn. To my daughter Joy and her husband Demarcus who are wonderful testimonies for Jesus. To my daughter Kimberly, who God has used to teach me many lessons.

To Andre, Deon, Love and Taylor my grandchildren, whose young lives have motivated me to write this book: so one day they can read of my Biblical theology. I hope they will be encouraged in their own personal Bible studies, along with all other grandchildren to come, as well as all others who may read this book.

Acknowledgment

Gracious thanks for this book go to
Vera Berry, Kathy Schlittenhart, Toni Webber, Lyndel Ford,
Merlyn Webber, Dr. James Leonard Elsman J.D.,
Dr. Sharon Stover, Bart Webber, Kimberly Dawn Webber,
Greg Gabriel, Professor Dr. Duane Dunham,
Deane Roloff.

TABLE OF CONTENTS

PREFACE

Early in my Christian studies and ministry, I found the need to write "sections" as a means of defense on topics that, in my opinion, were being either misrepresented or ignored by many. It was more efficient to hand someone my views on a subject, requesting them to read them, before the discussion developed. I would explain to them that they could help me out by taking a red pen and marking the paper up whenever they found apparent errors. Then we could get back together and talk about it. I found this method as a far more productive usage of time.

My Sections are ongoing projects in which I do not claim to be right on everything. I'm just saying that if I'm wrong, help me out in my misunderstanding.

Whether you agree or not, there is much one can learn from being exposed to this topic. Provoking Biblical thinking can't be all wrong.

In considering end-times events, there is much that can be known and much that cannot. Interpreting prophecy is difficult for many reasons, and one of them is the fact that there are mysterious events that are prophesied that do not become clearly understood until they happen.

I want to make clear to all who read this Book; I am not saying my positions are the way things are going to happen in the future. This is just my attempt to fit things together. I am probably wrong in areas. Yet maybe something can be gained through considering these issues from my point of view. No matter what approach one takes on this subject, there are difficult questions that can be asked. The answers are not always easily understood nor without speculation. My attempt is one of trying to eliminate more of the difficult problems than the other approaches do. One thing we can know for sure: this puzzle does fit perfectly together.

1

WHO IS CONFUSED?

I offer no guarantees that the prophets listed below actually made these predictions. I have described their alleged predictions as they were reported on the web, in newspapers, books, etc. I do not have the resources to track down original source material.

William Miller

A Baptist Minister in 1818, taught that Jesus Christ would return in 1843. His associates set October 22, 1844 as the final date when Jesus Christ would return.

A number of scholars of the day held similar views as Miller.

When Jesus did not return, Miller predicted this new date. In an event which is now called "The Great Disappointment," many Christians sold their property and possessions, quit their jobs and prepared themselves for the Second Coming. Nothing happened; the day came and went without incident.

Mrs. Ellen G. White

In her early career, Mrs. White made a number of predictions about Christ's imminent return. The most notable of those was a specific prediction made at a conference of believers in 1856. This statement was later published in the book *Testimonies* and received widespread attention within the Seventh Day Adventists Church. Mrs. White claimed that she was shown in a vision that some of those present at the 1856 conference would be translated:

I was shown the company present at the Conference. Said the angel: "Some food for worms, some subjects of the seven last plagues, some will be alive and remain upon the earth to be translated at the coming of Jesus." Testimonies, Vol. 1, p. 131

Mrs. White said she was given a vision showing the fate of those people attending the conference. She specifically states that some of them will suffer the seven last plagues, and some will be alive when Jesus returns. The Whites had such confidence in this "vision" that it was published in Mrs. White's *Testimonies to the Church* and received widespread distribution. However, by the early 1900s all those who attended the conference had passed away, leaving the Church with the dilemma of trying to figure out how to explain away such a prominent prophetic failure.

Joseph Smith

On 1835-FEB-14, Joseph Smith, the founder of the Mormon church, attended a meeting of church leaders. He said that the meeting had been called because God had commanded it. He announced that Jesus would return within 56 years -- *i.e. before 1891-FEB-15. (History of the Church 2:182) Obviously he was wrong.*

(Watchtower Bible and Tract Society)

1914 was one of the more important estimates of the start of the war of Armageddon by the Jehovah's Witnesses (Watchtower Bible and Tract Society). They based their prophecy of 1914 from prophecy in the book of Daniel, Chapter 4. The writings referred to "seven times". The WTS interpreted each "time" as equal to 360 days, giving a total of 2520 days. This was further interpreted as representing 2520 years, measured from the starting date of 607 BCE. This gave 1914 as the target date. When 1914 passed, they changed their prediction; 1914 became the year that Jesus invisibly began His rule.

1915, 1918, 1920, 1925, 1941, 1975 and 1994, etc. were other dates that the Watchtower Society (WTS) or its members predicted incorrectly.

Edgar C. Whisenant

(September 25, 1932 – May 16, 2001), was a former NASA engineer and Bible student who predicted the Rapture would occur in 1988, sometime between Sept. 11 and Sept. 13. He published two books about this: *88 Reasons Why the Rapture Will Be in 1988 and On Borrowed Time.* Eventually, 300,000 copies of *88 Reasons* were mailed free of charge to ministers across America, and 4.5 million copies were sold in bookstores and elsewhere. Whisenant was quoted as saying "Only if the Bible is in error am I wrong; and I say that to every preacher in town," and "If there were a king in this country and I could gamble with my life, I would stake my life on Rosh Hashana 88."

Whisenant's predictions were taken seriously in some parts of the evangelical Christian community. As the great day approached, regular programming on the Christian Trinity Broadcast Network (TBN) was interrupted to provide special instructions on preparing for the Rapture.

When the predicted Rapture failed to occur, Whisenant followed up with later books with predictions for various dates in 1989, 1993, and 1994. These books did not sell in quantity. Whisenant continued to issue various Rapture predictions through 1997, but gathered little attention.

Hal Lindsey

The Late, Great Planet Earth is the title of a best-selling 1970 book co-authored by Hal Lindsey and Carole C. Carlson, and first published by Zondervan.

Although Lindsey did not claim to know the dates of future events with any certainty, he suggested that Matthew 24:32-34 indicated that Jesus' return might be within "one generation" of the rebirth of the state of Israel, and the rebuilding of the Jewish Temple, and Lindsey asserted that "in the Bible" one generation is forty years. Some readers took this as an indication that the Tribulation or the Rapture would occur no later than 1988. In his 1980 work, The 1980s: *Countdown to Armageddon*, Lindsey predicted that "the decade of the 1980s could very well be the last decade of history as we know it."

Christians
Many Christians thought that the year 2000 was key to Biblical prophesy. They waited for catastrophe.

Harold Camping
According to Harold Camping, a Christian radio preacher, Jesus was coming back May 21, 2011. *It did not happen.*

Jesus said:
Matthew 24:36
"But of that day and hour no one knows, not even the angels of heaven, nor the Son, but the Father alone.

It's very difficult to explain with certainty the reasons why good men and woman are so zealous to predict the return of Jesus Christ.

We can know...

Matthew 24:11
"Many false prophets will arise and will mislead many.

I have found when it comes to end times events, people are dogmatic on all sorts of things, claiming the Antichrist to be the Pope or even Bill Clinton, and on and on it goes.

Last day's prophecies are important for many reasons and the blessings can be yours.

Revelation 1:3
Blessed is he who reads and those who hear the words of the prophecy, and heeds the things which are written in it; for the time is near.

Being ready
does not mean you have to have it all figured out.

I suggest you stick with the simple building blocks of Scripture and build with humility and flexibility in your understanding.

There is much that cannot be known with certainty until it actually happens.

The following simple illustration is what I'm getting at.

Matthew 24:3-4
As He was sitting on the Mount of Olives, the disciples came to Him privately, saying, "Tell us, when will these things happen, and what will be the sign of Your coming, and of the end of the age?"

Jesus' disciples asked some questions as a result of what Jesus had told them about the destruction of the Temple.

For example, why didn't Jesus respond like this:

The temple you see will be destroyed in about 40 years. But that won't be a great concern because not long from now, I am going to die for the sins of the world and be put in a tomb for 3 days. After this I will rise from the dead, then appear to people for 40 days and then I will ascend to heaven. A few days later, the New Covenant will take effect when the Holy Spirit will come to live within all believers. That starts the time period of the Church that will go on for thousands of years. There will be signs of my coming, which will be wars, famines, earthquakes, false prophets and false Christs, but these are just the birth pains. The Gospel will be preached all over the world. Then there will be a rapture of my Church and then a 7 year tribulation period where the Antichrist will appear. There will be many judgments by God during these 7 years. Then I will return and separate the sheep from the goats and the Millennium will begin for one thousand years where Satan will be bound till the very end; and finally, he will be unleashed and come out and make war against Me and I will defeat him and that will be the end. Lastly then there will be a final judgment called the Great White Throne Judgment. This Earth and Heaven you see will pass away and there will be a completely New Heaven and Earth, so always be ready.

The example I just gave to the disciples' question, was approximately 257 words; whereas Jesus' answer was over 1900 words. My question is: "which would appear to be clearer and more understandable, the example of 257 words or Jesus over 1900 words in Matthew 24-25?"

As a result of Jesus' answer to the disciples' question we have great difficulty understanding how and when things are going to occur, which should motivate us all to be ready at any time.

Whereas with my response to the disciples' question, it would appear to be clearer and more understandable. However, it could create complacence, taking away from the urgency of the message.

Even with Jesus' overall message of being ready at all times, we still have much of the Church far too worldly and self-centered, imbedded in materialism and sleeping.

Few chapters of the Bible have called forth more disagreement among interpreters than Matthew 24 and its parallels in Mark 13 and Luke 21. The history of the interpretation of this chapter is immensely complex. The literary nature of chapters 24-25 and of the parallels in Mark and Luke has occupied much scholarly attention.
(The Expositor's Bible Commentary, page 488)

Therefore, in this study, as with all others, take your time, check things out for yourself and be slow to be dogmatic about many of the unknowns within Biblical prophecy.

I see all of the current... positions on the order of last days events, as I would look at a table with three legs.

What I am doing with this book is adding a forth leg to take away the wobble.

So be patient as I build to the main point. First I demonstrate the lack of many in dealing with pertinent verses. Then I show the clarity of many of the prophetic verses. I then reveal the only options available for the prophetic verses within the normal Christian positions, and finally I reveal the problems and then on to my solution. Have fun!

2

BIBLICAL DUMP

We use trash bags to throw out our unwanted items. Many a Bible believer has his or her own biblical trash bag where he or she throws out unwanted verses and concepts. This is done in many different ways, but the bottom line is always the same: the unwanted verses go into the Biblical trash bag.

One problem is many do not do their own independent study of the Bible. Rather, they follow what others have come up with and pledge their allegiance to that.

I would not say other opinions are not important in growing in one's Biblical understanding; but I am one that dogmatically advocates not hanging your hat on another's hat rack.

Do your own studies, take your time and draw your own conclusions. If you're not willing to do that, then just stick with the simplicity of the Scriptures and keep silent about the roads you have not traveled.

One tactic commonly used to place things in the Biblical trash bag is simply ignoring the things you do not want to deal with, as if they don't exist. This becomes a very comfortable way of life for those who follow others.

Many positions are dogmatic and rigid going from point to point to their desired end conclusion. Some views go from the Tribulation to the Second Coming to the Millennium to the Great White Throne Judgment to the New Heavens and Earth.

Usually they disregard one of the most important times recorded within the Scriptures which has incredible implications and principles that do not usually play into their time frames nor understanding.

So let's take a look.

Revelation 20:7-9

When the thousand years are completed, Satan will be released from his prison, 8) and will come out to deceive the nations which are in the four corners of the earth, Gog and Magog, to gather them together for the war; the number of them is like the sand of the seashore. 9) And they came up on the broad plain of the earth and surrounded the camp of the saints and the beloved city, and fire came down from heaven and devoured them. (This refers to a time period.)

Note:

1. The thousand year Millennium is over.

2. Satan is released.

3. Satan goes out to deceive.
Who is he deceiving and what are his methods? What are the circumstances? Keep in mind the people he is deceiving have lived in a holy environment that has been going on for 1,000 years. How can he deceive them, knowing full well Jesus and the saints and angels are present as they have been for 1000 years?

4. Satan makes war. How, under the circumstances?
Again a time period has to be factored in.

5. The number of the deceived are like the sand on the seashore. How can this happen? What can we learn from this?

Why ignore this time period and many important principles?

Another position advocates that many prophetic events in scripture do not apply now simply because the events have already happened. One group discounts the whole book of Revelation by using this approach. They can sleep like a baby at night thinking they do not have to deal with the content of the book of Revelation.

Others can discount whole sections of Scriptures when they classify them as God's ideas that were never meant to happen. One such example is found in Ezekiel 40-48.
Many scholars of all kinds have no idea what the meaning or timing is of these chapters.

F. L. Anderson

Conception Unique and Ideal: While, however, there is this historical relation, it is to be observed that Ezekiel's temple-sketch is unique, presenting features not found in any of the actually built temples. The temple is, in truth, an ideal construction never intended to be literally realized by returned exiles, or any other body of people.

Visionary in origin, the ideas embodied, and not the actual construction, are the main things to the prophet's mind. It gives Ezekiel's conception of what a perfectly restored temple and the service of Yahweh would be under conditions which could scarcely be thought of as ever likely literally to arise. (F. L. Anderson, International Standard Bible Encyclopedia, pg. 2934-2935)

Let me introduce another type of Biblical trash bag. In this case, verses are not thrown away but just left as clutter.

Within last days prophecy there are many verses that pertain to Israel. I have found many people cram these prophecies into their preconceived positions without dealing with how the content plays out in real time, with real people, and real circumstances. This creates confusing clutter.

Christians separate last days events into different positions, and these positions often times cause separation between brothers. I am not condemning people for holding different positions. What I am suggesting is having proper attitudes towards fellow members of the body of Christ, while holding different positions.

Another area of concern is the lack of recognition that more than one truth or principal can be spoken of in different ways.

When this principal is not taken into consideration, truths can be trashed.

For example:
When a person is saved, the Holy Spirit enters that person's physical body.

He is in Christ and in the Father.
But where is He?
Is He in heaven or on earth?
In God, with God, where?
In the body or out of the body?
Is He in more than one place at the same time?

John 17:21
That they may all be one; even as You, Father, are in Me and I in You, **that they also may be in Us,** so that the world may believe that You sent Me.

Ephesians 2:5-6
Even when we were dead in our transgressions, made us alive together with Christ (by grace you have been saved), **6) and raised us up with Him, and seated us with Him in the heavenly places in Christ Jesus,**

2 Corinthians 12:2-4
I know a man in Christ who fourteen years ago - whether in the body I do not know, or out of the body I do not know, God knows - such a man was caught up to the third heaven. 3) And I know how such a man - whether in the body or apart from the body I do not know, God knows 4) was caught up into Paradise, and heard inexpressible words, which a man is not permitted to speak.

2 Corinthians 5:8
We are of good courage, I say, and prefer rather to be **absent from the body and to be at home with the Lord.**

1 Corinthians 15:42-44
So also is the resurrection of the dead. It is sown a perishable body, it is raised an imperishable body; 43) it is sown in dishonor, it is raised in glory; it is sown in weakness, it is raised in power; 44) it is sown a natural body, it is raised a spiritual body. If there is a natural body , there is also a spiritual body.

Examples like this in Scripture are used often within last days' prophecies. Verses can have more than one application.

There are also parallels. In other words, one verse can speak of two separate events. If we're not careful, we can be trying to place a round peg into a square hole.

Be careful and cautious as you determine for yourself what to believe about the end times.

Always remembering…

2 Timothy 3:16-17
All Scripture is inspired by God and profitable for teaching, for reproof, for correction, for training in righteousness; 17) so that the man of God may be adequate, equipped for every good work.

Nothing should end up in the trash bag.

3

CLEAR AS A BELL

Many people have the impression when it comes to verses on Bible prophecy that they are unclear and difficult to understand. So my intent with this chapter is to demonstrate through just one book of the Bible that is not always the case.

There are many prophesies that are clear as a bell. The question does not center around their clarity, but rather where and how you place them within your Last Days' prophecy position.
The following are some examples. Where would you place these events in your prophetic position?

Isaiah 1:26
"Then I will restore your judges as at the first, and your counselors as at the beginning; after that you will be called the city of righteousness, a faithful city."

Isaiah 2:2
Now it will come about that in the last days the mountain of the house of the LORD will be established as the chief of the mountains, and will be raised above the hills; and all the nations will stream to it.

Isaiah 2:12
For the LORD of hosts will have a day of reckoning against everyone who is proud and lofty and against everyone who is lifted up, that he may be abased.

Isaiah 4:1
For seven women will take hold of one man in that day, saying, "We will eat our own bread and wear our own clothes, only let us be called by your name; take away our reproach!"

Isaiah 9:6
For a child will be born to us, a son will be given to us; and the government will rest on His shoulders; and His name will be called Wonderful Counselor, Mighty God, Eternal Father, Prince of Peace.

Isaiah 11:6
And the wolf will dwell with the lamb, And the leopard will lie down with the young goat, And the calf and the young lion and the fatling together; and a little boy will lead them.

Isaiah 13:5-6
They are coming from a far country, From the farthest horizons, The LORD and His instruments of indignation, to destroy the whole land. 6) Judgment on the Day of the LORD. Wail, for the day of the LORD is near! It will come as destruction from the Almighty.

Isaiah 19:23
In that day there will be a highway from Egypt to Assyria, and the Assyrians will come into Egypt and the Egyptians into Assyria, and the Egyptians will worship with the Assyrians.

Isaiah 25:6
The LORD of hosts will prepare a lavish banquet for all peoples on this mountain; A banquet of aged wine, choice pieces with marrow, and refined, aged wine.

Isaiah 26:19
Your dead will live; their corpses will rise. You who lie in the dust, awake and shout for joy, For your dew is as the dew of the dawn, and the earth will give birth to the departed spirits.

Isaiah 30:26
The light of the moon will be as the light of the sun, and the light of the sun will be seven times brighter, like the light of seven days, on the day the LORD binds up the fracture of His people and heals the bruise He has inflicted.

Isaiah 31:8
And the Assyrian will fall by a sword not of man, and a sword not of man will devour him. So he will not escape the sword, and his young men will become forced laborers.

Isaiah 32:1
Behold, a king will reign righteously and princes will rule justly.

Isaiah 33:7
Behold, their brave men cry in the streets, the ambassadors of peace weep bitterly.

Isaiah 34:2
For the LORD'S indignation is against all the nations, and His wrath against all their armies; He has utterly destroyed them, He has given them over to slaughter.

Isaiah 35:5-6
Then the eyes of the blind will be opened and the ears of the deaf will be unstopped. 6) Then the lame will leap like a deer, and the tongue of the mute will shout for joy. For waters will break forth in the wilderness and streams in the Arabah.

Isaiah 40:10
Behold, the Lord GOD will come with might, with His arm ruling for Him. Behold, His reward is with Him and His recompense before Him.

Isaiah 43:5
"Do not fear, for I am with you; I will bring your offspring from the east, and gather you from the west.

Isaiah 45:23
"I have sworn by Myself, the word has gone forth from My mouth in righteousness and will not turn back, that to Me every knee will bow, every tongue will swear allegiance.

Isaiah 51:6
" Lift up your eyes to the sky, then look to the earth beneath; For the sky will vanish like smoke, and the earth will wear out like a garment and its inhabitants will die in like manner; but My salvation will be forever, and My righteousness will not wane.

Isaiah 52:8
Listen! Your watchmen lift up their voices, they shout joyfully together; for they will see with their own eyes when the LORD restores Zion.

Isaiah 54:9
"For this is like the days of Noah to Me, when I swore that the waters of Noah would not flood the earth again; so I have sworn that I will not be angry with you nor will I rebuke you.

Isaiah 60:1-3
"Arise, shine; for your light has come, and the glory of the LORD has risen upon you. 2) "For behold, darkness will cover the earth and deep darkness the peoples; but the LORD will rise upon you and His glory will appear upon you. 3) "Nations will come to your light, and kings to the brightness of your rising.

Isaiah 61:4

Then they will rebuild the ancient ruins, they will raise up the former devastations; and they will repair the ruined cities, the desolations of many generations.

Isaiah 62:11

Behold, the LORD has proclaimed to the end of the earth, say to the daughter of Zion, "Lo, your salvation comes; behold His reward is with Him, and His recompense before Him."

Isaiah 63:1

Who is this who comes from Edom, with garments of glowing colors from Bozrah, this One who is majestic in His apparel, marching in the greatness of His strength? "It is I who speak in righteousness, mighty to save."

Isaiah 65:16

"Because he who is blessed in the earth will be blessed by the God of truth; and he who swears in the earth will swear by the God of truth; because the former troubles are forgotten, and because they are hidden from My sight!

Isaiah 66:12-13

For thus says the LORD, "Behold, I extend peace to her like a river, and the glory of the nations like an overflowing stream; and you will be nursed, you will be carried on the hip and fondled on the knees. 13) "As one whom his mother comforts, so I will comfort you; and you will be comforted in Jerusalem."

Again, the issue does not center around the clarity of Scriptures, but rather where and how they are placed.

It's not always easy to determine where they belong in God's prophetic time table.

Another interesting concept to consider is how they were given. Were they given in a linear chronological order?

Could they have been given as if one were to view a mural moving from place to place, without regard for order or timing?

These are issues that need to be taken into consideration in rightly dividing the Scriptures in order for one to determine his own Last Days position.

4

WHICH VIEW?

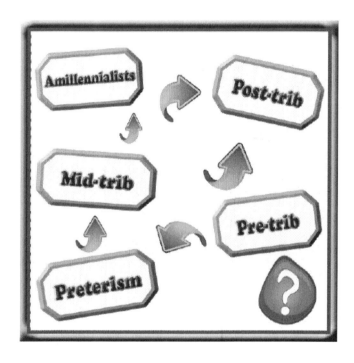

There is no requirement for a person to make a final determination on Bible prophecy. Yet all Christian views on biblical prophecy should be examined. Hopefully someone has got it right. In this chapter, I will discuss the different ways to view End Time events in Revelation and other prophetic passages.

1. **Amillennialists believe:** The end times are figurative and will not be literally fulfilled on the earth: no 1000 year millennium on the earth.

The Bible

does use figurative language, and when used is intended to have literal meaning; otherwise you're left with nothing more than dust in the wind.

Dr. Duane Dunham,
Professor NT Greek and Exegesis, Western Conservative Baptist Seminary, 29 years:
"Figures of speech are not to hide the truth but to heighten the truth."

Some amillennialists try to support their belief with:

2 Peter 3:10
which says, "But the day of the Lord will come as a thief in the night; in which the heavens shall pass away with great noise, and the elements shall melt with fervent heat, the earth also and the works that are therein shall be burned up."

Amillennialists say the earth is destroyed immediately after the rapture in one day. They actually use this verse to support their view.

However, they fail to check the context of the passage. Just two verses before, Peter said, *"But, beloved, be not ignorant of this one thing, that one day is with the Lord as a thousand years, and a thousand years as one day."* (**2 Peter 3:8**).
(Some Amillennialists even use this verse to try to prove that the 1000 years mentioned in Revelation 20:1-7 are not a literal 1000 years.)

The Day of the Lord: Represents a time period starting with the last trumpet of 1 Corinthians 15:52 and extends through to the end of the millennium in my opinion. Otherwise, we might as well take a black marker and start blotting verses out of the Bible.

Revelation 22:18-19
I testify to everyone who hears the words of the prophecy of this book: if anyone adds to them, God will add to him the plagues which are written in this book; **19) and if anyone takes away from the words of the book of this prophecy,** God will take away his part from the tree of life and from the holy city, which are written in this book.

2. **The Post-Trib position:** Believes the Rapture will not occur until the end of the seven - year Tribulation, just prior to the beginning of the Millennium kingdom.

The Post-Trib position has a real problem when it comes to populating the Millennial kingdom, because they advocate that the second coming of Christ and the Rapture as practically simultaneous. If all believers are raptured at the end of the Tribulation, who will be left to populate the earth during the Millennium?

A.) (Rapture) All believers are caught up to meet Jesus in the sky. 1 Corinthians 15:52 -1 Thessalonians 4:17

B.) (Rapture) All believers receive their spiritual bodies.

1 Corinthians 15:42-44
So also is the resurrection of the dead. It is sown a perishable body, it is raised an imperishable body; 43) it is sown in dishonor, it is raised in glory; it is sown in weakness, it is raised in power; 44) it is sown a natural body, it is raised a spiritual body. If there is a natural body, there is also a spiritual body.

C.) <u>At the Second Coming</u> Jesus comes down to the earth and separates the sheep from the goats before the millennium starts.

Matthew 25:31-35
"But when the Son of Man comes in His glory, and all the angels with Him, then He will sit on His glorious throne. 32) "All the nations will be gathered before Him; and He will separate them from one another, as the shepherd separates the sheep from the goats; 33) and He will put the sheep on His right, and the goats on the left. 34) "Then the King will say to those on His right, 'Come, you who are blessed of My Father, inherit the kingdom prepared for you from the foundation of the world.

Matthew 25:41
"Then He will also say to those on His left, ' Depart from Me, accursed ones, into the eternal fire which has been prepared for the devil and his angels;

The Post-Trib position does not allow for the separation of the sheep and goats on earth by Jesus after His Second Coming.

Here's the problem: If the Rapture catches away all of the believers at Christ's second coming, then there will be no "sheep" left to be in the judgment of the sheep and the goats (Matt 25), which must happen before the Millennium.

Also, we know that after the second coming, during the Battle of Armageddon, Jesus and the armies of heaven will fight the antichrist and the millions of soldiers from the nations. Jesus is going to be the Victor, and He is going to cast them all (the antichrist, false prophet, the kings of the earth and their armies) into the Lake of Fire.

Then, according to Revelation 19:21 that seems to correspond with Matt 25:41 referring to the same time: it says, "and the rest were killed with the sword which came from the mouth of Him who sat on the horse [Jesus]..." Who are "the rest"? It seems they have to be all of the remaining unrighteous people from the nations (the goats) who have survived the Tribulation, but were not in the armies of the antichrist, because all of the armies have already been destroyed and cast away into the Lake of Fire.

Where do we find the mortals to populate the Millennium?

So, the real fallacy in the argument of the Post-Trib position is this: if all of the Tribulation saints have been raptured and given their heavenly bodies at Jesus' second coming, and all of the unrighteous Tribulation survivors have been killed by the Lord Jesus Christ, <u>where are the human beings who will go through the judgment of the sheep and the goats Matt 25, and who will enter the Millennium?</u>
Where are the sheep?

43

According to the Post-Trib position there would not be any human beings left! All human beings will either have been raptured at the second coming or will be in the Lake of Fire.

Prophecy students and scholars agree that the Millennium will be populated by actual human beings like us. People who hold to the Post-Trib position have no reasonable explanation for this inconsistency in their argument!

3. The Mid-Trib position: Believes that the Rapture will occur approximately three and one half years into the Tribulation.

Upon whom will the antichrist wage war? The antichrist will wage war on the believers immediately after the second half of the Tribulation. If all the believers had just been Raptured, there would be no saints left upon earth to wage war against.

Revelation 13:7
It was also given to him to make war with the saints and to overcome them, and authority over every tribe and people and tongue and nation was given to him.

The Mid-Trib position would require that half way into the Tribulation all believers would be removed. Therefore, within the second 3 1/2 years, a whole new start for the world of personal conversions would have to begin. That's in order for the antichrist to wage war against the saints.

Does it make sense God would remove one group of believers half way into the Tribulation, only to immediately have another group of believers come into being for the Tribulation?

4. The Pre-Trib position: Believes that the Rapture will occur prior to the seven year Tribulation, but not necessarily immediately before the Tribulation.

Personally, I believe in the Pre-Trib Rapture position. It's not the purpose of this Book to promote and defend that position. Yet, I do feel obligated to address a few issues. If someone would like to examine the many reasons why I choose to believe in the Pre-Trib Rapture position, they can obtain my book "Word Power" at: **http://www.amazon.com/**
In the search box, type in, the title by James Webber,
For example: Word Power by James Webber

One of the problems raised by the critics of the Pre-Trib Rapture position is that the trumpet in 1 Corinthians 15:52 is identified as "the last trumpet." Since the timing of the Pre-Trib rapture position is before the Great Tribulation, and since trumpets are sounded during the time of the Tribulation in the book of Revelation, the last trumpet I Corinthians 15:52 cannot be sounded before the trumpets in the book of Revelation.

In response:

Matthew 24:36 says no one knows the day of Jesus Christ's return.

Matthew 24:31
"And He will send forth His angels with A GREAT TRUMPET and THEY WILL GATHER TOGETHER His elect from the four winds, from one end of the sky to the other.

Matthew 24:36
"But of <u>that day and hour</u> no one knows, not even the angels of heaven, nor the Son, but the Father alone.

(Matthew 24:36 has to be speaking of the Rapture as "the last trumpet" since it would be easy to calculate the coming of the Son of Man to the very day otherwise.)

The Second Coming of Jesus is a separate event that is exactly 7 years from the appearing of the Antichrist and 1,260 days from the appearance of the Abomination of Desolation standing in the holy place. (Matthew 24:15 Daniel 9:27)

With this understanding, it's easy to see the important distinctions between the "last trumpet" (Rapture) and the Second Coming.

No one can know the time of the Rapture "last trumpet", but we can know the very day of the Second Coming "trumpet". This shows a clear differences between the two events.

With the one view people are looking for: the return of Jesus Christ, 1 Corinthians 15:52.
And with the other view people are looking for: the appearance of the Antichrist.

Matthew 24:15-16
"Therefore **when you see** the ABOMINATION OF DESOLATION which was spoken of through Daniel the prophet, standing in the holy place (let the reader understand), 16) then those who are in Judea must flee to the mountains.

What is the "last trumpet" of 1 Corinthians 15:52 referring to?

I personally do not think it's a stretch to assume that "the last trumpet" of 1 Corinthians 15:52 is the trumpet call signifying the start of the end times and the removal of the Body of Christ 1 Thessalonians 4:16. There are other trumpets that follow but by their nature they are of a different type. Every series has a last. For example: School is out at the last bell, but every day of the school year there is a last bell.

Keep in mind what is said to be happening just before the last trumpet of 1 Corinthians 15:52, where the Church is removed, which is not plausible just before the Second Coming:

Matthew 24:37-41
"For the coming of the Son of Man will be just like the days of Noah. 38) "For as in those days before the flood they were eating and drinking, marrying and giving in marriage, until the day that Noah entered the ark, **39) and they did not understand until the flood came and took them all away; so will the coming of the Son of Man be.** 40) "Then there will be two men in the field; one will be taken and one will be left. 41) " Two women will be grinding at the mill; one will be taken and one will be left.

It's not reasonable to think that the few remaining people of the earth prior to the Second Coming are going to be partying, eating, drinking, marrying and given in marriage like in the days of Noah without understanding, disregarding what had just happened (The Great Tribulation) -- Seven Seals, Seven Trumpets, and Seven Bowls, etc. Otherwise, God's wrath would seem to be ineffectual.

It's more reasonable for people to be eating and drinking and partying before the Tribulation starts.

Keep in mind the conditions prior to the Second Coming:

Matthew 24:22
"And unless those days had been cut short, no life would have been saved; but for the sake of the elect those days shall be cut short."

**This is just one of the many contrasting differences
showing that the removing of the Church,
1 Corinthians 15:52 - 1 Thessalonians 4:17, is a different
event than that of the Second Coming, Matthew 25:31.**

5. **Preterism is:** A eschatological view that interprets prophecies as events which have already happened in the first century A.D.

There are two groups of preterists, the one called partial preterism and the other full preterism.

Partial preterism holds that most eschatological prophecies, such as the destruction of Jerusalem, the Antichrist, the Great Tribulation, and the advent of the Day of the Lord as a "judgment-coming" of Christ were fulfilled in A.D. 70 during the persecution of Christians under the Emperor Nero.

The Second coming and the resurrection of the dead, however, have not yet occurred in the partial preterist system.

Full preterism differs from partial preterism in that full preterist believe that all eschatology or "end time" events were fulfilled with the destruction of Jerusalem, including the resurrection of the dead and Jesus' Second Coming.

Partial preterism advocates:

•We are in the "millennium" (Kingdom) now as Christ's Kingdom is being extended through the preaching of His Gospel.

•The Devil is bound now, but will seek to deceive the nations and be condemned to the Lake of Fire at the culmination of time.

Full preterism advocates:

•The Millennium is a past event which occurred between 26AD and 66AD (40 years from the date of the crucifixion).

•The Devil was cast into the Lake of Fire in 70 AD.

Problems

A few of the many problems with the preterist position are:

In order to make 70 AD the magic year, we would have to delete dozens of prophecies that were never fulfilled.

When was the Gospel preached to all the nations?

When was the mark of the Beast implemented?

5

THE PROBLEM

I want to make clear to all who read this book; I am not saying my positions are the way things are going to happen in the future. This is just my attempt to fit things together. I am probably wrong in areas. Yet maybe something can be gained through considering these issues from my point of view. No matter what approach one takes on this subject, there are difficult questions that can be asked. The answers are not always easily understood nor without speculation. My attempt is one of trying to eliminate more of the difficult problems than the other approaches do. One thing we can know for sure: this puzzle does fit perfectly together.

**Interpreting prophecy** is difficult for many reasons and one of them is the fact that there are mysterious events that are prophesied that do not become clearly understood until they happen.

Regardless of one's view of last day prophecy, there are a number of verses within the Bible that have to be addressed. The method one uses to interpret these verses will determine the outcome, which can be diverse in content and application.

With this understanding, let's take a look at some verses.

Ezekiel 38:14
"Therefore prophesy, son of man, and say to Gog, 'Thus says the Lord GOD, "On that day when My people Israel are living securely, will you not know it?

In Ezekiel 38:14 when it says:
"Thus says the Lord GOD,"
I choose to believe it's speaking of the same God identified in **2 Peter 1:21,** _for no prophecy was ever made by an act of human will, but men moved by the Holy Spirit spoke from God._

Therefore, I place importance on the words with literal meanings and when I find figurative language being used, I give it a literal meaning when possible. Sometimes it may not be possible simply because the literal application has not been revealed yet.

When it says in **Ezekiel 38:14** "On that day when **My people Israel are living securely,"** is that speaking of a past time, a present time, or a future time?

It says in **Ezekiel 38: 15-16,** " You will come from your place out of the remote parts of the north, you and many peoples with you, all of them riding on horses, a great assembly and a mighty army; 16) and you will come up against My people Israel like a cloud to cover the land. **It shall come about in the Last Days that I will bring you against My land,** so that the nations may know Me when I am sanctified through you before their eyes, O Gog."

Are verses 15-16 speaking of a past time, a present time or a future time? Verse **16** says, "It shall come about in the **last days.**" That's a good indicator that the verse is referring to a future time.

The question is, how does **Ezekiel 38:15-16** fit into the prophetic positions revealed within Chapter 4.

Let's look at some of the rest of the content in Ezekiel chapter 38-39 to see if we can find where it fits.

We see in **Ezekiel 38:18-23** "It will come about **on that day,** when Gog comes against the land of Israel," declares the Lord GOD, "that My fury will mount up in My anger. 19) "In My zeal and in My blazing wrath I declare that on that day there will surely be a great earthquake in the land of Israel. 20) "The fish of the sea, the birds of the heavens, the beasts of the field, all the creeping things that creep on the earth, and all the men who are on the face of the earth will shake at My presence; the mountains also will be thrown down, the steep pathways will collapse and every wall will fall to the ground. 21) "I will call for a sword against him on all My mountains," declares the Lord GOD. " Every man's sword will be against his brother.

22) "With pestilence and with blood I will enter into judgment with him; and I will rain on him and on his troops, and on the many peoples who are with him, a torrential rain, with hailstones, fire and brimstone. 23) "I will magnify Myself, sanctify Myself, and make Myself known in the sight of many nations; and they will know that I am the LORD.'"

The description given in **Ezekiel 38:18-23** is incredible. I believe in past Biblical history, it can only be trumped by the great Flood.

The question is, where does it fit?
Does it fit in the 7 year Great Tribulation or in a time between the Second Coming and the starting of the Millennium? Or is it referring to a time after the Millennium before the Great White Throne Judgment?

To help us try to determine that, we will look at a few more verses that deal with the result of Ezekiel 38:18-23.

Ezekiel 39:9
"Then those who inhabit the cities of Israel will go out and make fires with the weapons and burn them, both shields and bucklers, bows and arrows, war clubs and spears, **and for seven years they will make fires of them.**

Ezekiel 39:12
"**For seven months** the house of Israel will be burying them in order to cleanse the land.

We have here a case of Israelis destroying the weapons that were mounted against them for seven years indicating the magnitude of the force that came against them. It takes them seven months just to bury the dead.

Again we ask the question within the positions of Chapter 4: where do these events fit?

During the 7 year Great Tribulation or in a time between the second coming and the starting of the Millennium, or is it referring to a time after the Millennium before the Great White Throne Judgment?

Do they fit within the mid-trib position?

"In examining these arguments for a mid-tribulation fulfillment of Ezekiel 38-39, the following observations are noted:

1. There is no specific basis in the Biblical text for equating Gog with the king of the north.

2. A concept of "false security" and prosperity (38:11-12) are both inconsistent with the purpose of the Tribulation (a time of Israel's chastisement and punishment) and contrary to the usual meaning of the phrase "live safely" in Ezekiel 38-39 (a millennial concept).

3. The cleansing of the land through burning weapons and burying bodies for seven years and seven months, respectively, would seem inconceivable during the Abomination of Desolation, when judgment is at its height.

4. Ezekiel 38:8 declares that Israel has been restored from the sword into Messianic blessing; yet this would be incongruous with the Tribulation period.

5. Ezekiel 38-39 clearly points out that it is God who destroys Gog, not the Antichrist.

6. Ezekiel's assertions (39:7, 22, 25) that the Lord's name would never again be profaned among the nations seem antithetical with the Tribulation period. Therefore, it seems questionable that the events of Ezekiel 38-39 transpire in the middle of the Tribulation."

(THE EXPOSITOR'S BIBLE COMMENTARY Vol 6 page 939)

Where do these verses fit?

Ezekiel 39:9

"Then those who inhabit the cities of Israel will go out and make fires with the weapons and burn them, both shields and bucklers, bows and arrows, war clubs and spears, and for **seven years** they will make fires of them.

Ezekiel 39:12

"For **seven months** the house of Israel will be burying them in order to cleanse the land.

Would they fit after the 1000 year Millennium?

Revelation 20:9-11

And they came up on the broad plain of the earth and surrounded the camp of the saints and the beloved city, and fire came down from heaven and devoured them. 10) And the devil who deceived them was thrown into the lake of fire and brimstone, where the beast and the false prophet are also; and they will be tormented day and night forever and ever. 11) then I saw a great white throne and Him who sat upon it, from whose presence earth and heaven fled away, and no place was found for them.

This option would require a 7 year time gap for clean up Ezekiel 39:9, between the destruction verse 9 and the Great White Throne Judgment in verse 11, which is not reasonable.

Plus: one of the main outcomes of Ezekiel 38-39 is that Israel and the nations would come to know that God is the God of Israel. (**Ezekiel 39:22**) "And the house of Israel will know that I am the LORD their God from that day onward.

But that is precisely what would have been going on for a thousand years prior to the destruction.

We are able to see Ezekiel 38-39 does not fit at the end of the Millennium.

Moving on to another most important issue.

In order to appreciate the magnitude of the point to be made, great importance has to be placed on the following verses:

Hebrews 9:15-17
For this reason He is the mediator of a new covenant, so that, since a death has taken place for the redemption of the transgressions that were committed under the first covenant, those who have been called may receive the promise of the eternal inheritance. 16) For where a covenant is, **there must of necessity be the death of the one who made it.** 17) For a covenant is valid only when men are dead, for it is never in force while the one who made it lives.

Ephesians 2:15-16
...by abolishing in His flesh the enmity, which is the Law of commandments contained in ordinances, **so that in Himself He might make the two into one new man,** thus establishing peace, 16) and might reconcile them both in one body to God through the cross, by it having put to death the enmity.

Colossians 2:14
having **canceled out** the certificate of debt consisting of decrees against us, which was hostile to us; and He has taken it out of the way, having nailed it to the cross.

Hebrews 7:16
who has become such not on the basis of a law of physical requirement, but according to the power of an indestructible life.

Hebrews 8:13
When He said, " A new covenant," **He has made the first obsolete.** But whatever is becoming obsolete and growing old is ready to disappear.

Hebrews 10:1
For the Law, since it has only a **shadow** of the good things to come and not the very form of things, **can never,** by the same sacrifices which they offer continually year by year, make perfect those who draw near.

Galatians 6:15
For neither is **circumcision** anything, nor **uncircumcision,** but a new creation.

Hebrews 7:26-27
For it was fitting for us to have such a high priest, holy, innocent, undefiled, separated from sinners and exalted above the heavens; 27) who does not need daily, like those high priests, to offer up sacrifices, first for His own sins and then for the sins of the people, **because this He did once for all when He offered up Himself.**

These verses are the very life blood of the Gospel of the Lord Jesus Christ. Jesus Christ, the Messiah, was the full and final sacrifice. He will not be offering more sacrifices in the future. He is our foundation and life.

Considering this fact, I ask the question, is the Ezekiel Temple with it's animal sacrifices in the time of the 1000 year Millennium? In Ezekiel 40-48 we find a Temple, it centers around Judaism. Many teachers of last days prophecy place the Ezekiel Temple in the 1000 year Millennium.

The book of Revelation speaks of the Millennium.

Revelation 20:1-3
Then I saw an angel coming down from heaven, holding the key of the abyss and a great chain in his hand. 2) And he laid hold of the dragon, **the serpent of old, who is the devil and Satan, and bound him for a thousand years;** 3) and he threw him into the abyss, and shut it and sealed it over him, so that he would not deceive the nations any longer, **until the thousand years were completed;** after these things he must be released for a short time.

Now we're faced with a problem; are these verses myth? Or do they have literal application?

I believe these verses are to be taken literally indicating there will be a 1000 year period we call the Millennium. The Millennium is the time in which many want to place Ezekiel 40-48.

The Millennium is the time where Revelation 20:6 says **Jesus Christ will reign.**

The Millennium is the time many believe that mortals will be repopulating the earth. It is where the Body of Christ, along with Old Testament resurrected saints and even angels will be, with Jesus Christ reigning over all.

(Paul the apostle is expected to be there.)
The Apostle Paul wrote:

Galatians 3:16-18
Now the promises were spoken to Abraham and to his seed. He does not say, "And to seeds," as referring to many, but rather to one. "And to your seed," that is, Christ. 17) What I am saying is this: the Law, which came four hundred and thirty years later, does not invalidate a covenant previously ratified by God, so as to nullify the promise. 18) For if the inheritance is based on law, it is no longer based on a promise; but God has granted it to Abraham by means of a promise.

Galatians 3:23-29
But before faith came, we were kept in custody under the law, being shut up to the faith which was later to be revealed. 24) Therefore the Law has become our tutor to lead us to Christ, so that we may be justified by faith. **25) But now that faith has come, we are no longer under a tutor.** 26) For you are all sons of God through faith in Christ Jesus. 27) For all of you who were baptized into Christ have clothed yourselves with Christ. **28) There is neither Jew nor Greek,** there is neither slave nor free man, there is neither male nor female; **for you are all one in Christ Jesus.** 29) And if you belong to Christ, then you are Abraham's descendants, heirs according to promise.

Galatians 5:1-6
It was for freedom that Christ set us free; therefore keep standing firm and **do not** be subject again to a yoke of slavery. **2) Behold I, Paul, say to you that if you receive circumcision, Christ will be of no benefit to you.** 3) And I testify again to every man who receives circumcision, that he is under obligation to keep the whole Law.

4) You have been severed from Christ, you who are seeking to be justified by law; you have fallen from grace. 5) For we through the Spirit, by faith, are waiting for the hope of righteousness. **6) For in Christ Jesus neither circumcision nor uncircumcision means anything, but faith working through love.**

<u>Anyone who loves and understands the finished work of Jesus Christ on the cross that is reflected within the verses above can understand how repulsive it is to place Ezekiel 40-48 in the Millennium where Jesus Christ is reigning with the Body of Christ.</u>

Dr. John C. Whitcomb writes,
A careful reading of Ezekiel 40-42 gives one the clear impression of a future literal Temple for Israel because of the immense number of details concerning its dimensions, its parts and its contents (see Erich Sauer, From Eternity To Eternity, chapter 34). Surely, if so much space in the Holy Scriptures is given to a detailed description of this Temple, we are safe in assuming that it will be as literal as the Tabernacle and the Temple of Solomon."
http://www.whitcombministries.org/Biblical_Articles/The_Millennial_Temple_Of_Ezekiel_40-48.php

Wellhausen has said that chapters 40-48 of Ezekiel "are the most important in his book, and have been, not incorrectly, called the key to the Old Testament..." *(Prolegomena, English translation, 167).*

**Note: within Ezekiel chapters 40-48 there is no mention of the Jewish Messiah, Jesus Christ, and His atoning sacrifice for sins. Nor is there any allusion to the fact that anything had been done for Israel by Jesus Christ. Nor is there even a hint that Jesus Christ is physically here on earth reigning in person. These facts make it very improbable that Ezekiel 40-48 occur during the Millennium.**

What we do have in Ezekiel 40-48 is animal sacrifices.
Ezekiel 43:18-19
And He said to me, " Son of man, thus says the Lord GOD, "These are the statutes for the altar on the day it is built, **to offer burnt offerings on it and to sprinkle blood on it.** 19) 'You shall give to the Levitical priests who are from the offspring of Zadok, who draw near to Me to minister to Me,' declares the Lord GOD, **'a young bull for a sin offering.**

We also have circumcision used as a means of division.
Ezekiel 44:9
"Thus says the Lord GOD, " No foreigner uncircumcised in heart and uncircumcised in flesh, of all the foreigners who are among the sons of Israel, shall enter My sanctuary.

They will bear their own sin.
Ezekiel 44:13
"And they shall not come near to Me to serve as a priest to Me, nor come near to any of My holy things, to the things that are most holy; but they will bear their shame and their abominations which they have committed.

No transmission of Holiness.
Ezekiel 44:19

"When they go out into the outer court, into the outer court to the people, they shall put off their garments in which they have been ministering and lay them in the holy chambers; then they shall put on other garments so that they will not transmit holiness to the people with their garments.

No head shaving.
Ezekiel 44:20

"Also they shall not shave their heads, yet they shall not let their locks grow long; they shall only trim the hair of their heads.

No wine.
Ezekiel 44:21

Nor shall any of the priests drink wine when they enter the inner court.

Only virgins, no divorced women.
Ezekiel 44:22

"And they shall not marry a widow or a divorced woman but shall take virgins from the offspring of the house of Israel, or a widow who is the widow of a priest.

There will be the clean and the unclean.
Ezekiel 44:23

"Moreover, they shall teach My people the difference between the holy and the profane, and cause them to discern between the unclean and the clean.

They will teach and judge and follow the Law.
Ezekiel 44:23-24
"Moreover, they shall **teach** My people the difference between the holy and the profane, and cause them to discern between the unclean and the clean. 24) "In a dispute they shall take their stand **to judge;** they shall judge it according to My ordinances. They shall also keep My laws and My statutes in all My appointed feasts and sanctify My sabbaths.

(Note: This is quite different from the Millennial Kingdom where Jesus is the teacher and the Judge.)

Isaiah 2:2-4 Now it will come about that in the last days the mountain of the house of the LORD will be established as the chief of the mountains, and will be raised above the hills; And all the nations will stream to it. 3) And many peoples will come and say, "Come, let us go up to the mountain of the LORD, To the house of the God of Jacob; **that He may teach** us concerning His ways And that we may walk in His paths." For the law will go forth from Zion and the word of the LORD from Jerusalem. 4) **and He will judge** between the nations, And will render decisions for many peoples; and they will hammer their swords into plowshares and their spears into pruning hooks. Nation will not lift up sword against nation, and never again will they learn war.

They will have to be clean.
Ezekiel 44:26
"After he is cleansed, seven days shall elapse for him."

They will make their sin offerings.
Ezekiel 44:27
"On the day that he goes into the sanctuary, into the inner court to minister in the sanctuary, he shall offer his sin offering," declares the Lord GOD.

There will be guilt offerings.
Ezekiel 44:29
"They shall eat the grain offering, the sin offering and the guilt offering; and every devoted thing in Israel shall be theirs."

The prince gets the offerings.
Ezekiel 45:16
"All the people of the land shall give to this offering for the prince in Israel.

The prince is in charge.
Ezekiel 45:17
"It shall be the prince's part to provide the burnt offerings, the grain offerings and the drink offerings, at the feasts, on the new moons and on the sabbaths, at all the appointed feasts of the house of Israel; he shall provide the sin offering, the grain offering, the burnt offering and the peace offerings, to make atonement for the house of Israel."

Sinners will need atonement.
Ezekiel 45:20
"Thus you shall do on the seventh day of the month for everyone who goes astray or is naive; so you shall make atonement for the house.

The prince sins.
Ezekiel 45:22
"On that day the prince shall provide for himself and all the people of the land a bull for a sin offering.

(**Note:** This picture in Ezekiel is quite different (with all the sinning going on), than the picture painted by Dwight Pentecost) *in His Book "THINGS TO COME" speaking of the Millennium Kingdom, page 488.*

"Holiness. The theocratic kingdom will be a holy kingdom, in which holiness is manifested through the King and King's subjects. The land will be holy, the city holy, the temple holy, **and the subjects holy unto the Lord,** Isaiah 4:3 It will come about that he who is left in Zion and remains in Jerusalem will be called holy — **everyone** who is recorded for life in Jerusalem. Isaiah 60:21 **"Then all your people will be righteous;** they will possess the land forever, the branch of My planting, the work of My hands, that I may be glorified.)

The prince has sons.
Ezekiel 46:16-17
'Thus says the Lord GOD, "If the prince gives a gift out of his inheritance **to any of his sons,** it shall belong to his sons; it is their possession by inheritance. 17) "But if he gives a gift from his inheritance to one of his servants, it shall be his until the year of liberty; then it shall return to the prince. His inheritance shall be only his sons'; it shall belong to them.

Holiness is not to be transmitted.
Ezekiel 46:20
He said to me, "This is the place where the priests shall boil the guilt offering and the sin offering and where they shall bake the grain offering, in order that they may not bring them out into the outer court to transmit holiness to the people."

The 12 tribes will be there.
Ezekiel 47:13
Thus says the Lord GOD, "This shall be the boundary by which you shall divide the land for an inheritance among the twelve tribes of Israel; Joseph shall have two portions.

Aliens will be there.
Ezekiel 47:22-23
"You shall divide it by lot for an inheritance among yourselves and among the aliens who stay in your midst, who bring forth sons in your midst. And they shall be to you as the native-born among the sons of Israel; they shall be allotted an inheritance with you among the tribes of Israel. 23) "And in the tribe with which the alien stays, there you shall give him his inheritance," declares the Lord GOD.

The prince will own property.
Ezekiel 48:22
"Exclusive of the property of the Levites and the property of the city, which are in the middle of that which belongs to the prince, everything between the border of Judah and the border of Benjamin shall be for the prince.

**Zechariah 14:9** is a reference to the Millennium and is quite different than Ezekiel 40-48

Zechariah 14:9
And the LORD will be king over all the earth; in that day the LORD will be the **only one,** and His name the **only one.**

We can see... Ezekiel 40-48 is inconsistent with the New Covenant and also the picture of the Millennial Kingdom.

**Some take the position that the Old Testament prophecies made to Israel have to be literally fulfilled.**

So they dump them into the Millennium.

Some of the same people claim the sacrifices of Ezekiel 40-48 are inefficacious.

Ralph H. Alexander, addressing Ezekiel 40-48, says: These rituals of atonement were commemorative of the finished work of Christ for sin through the sacrifice of Himself. They were not efficacious.
(The Expositor's Bible Commentary, Vol 6 p.g. 983)

What we have with their position during the Millennium is God's promises to Israel being fulfilled through ineffectual literal fulfilment.

Note: There is no mention of Jesus Christ and His atonement within Ezekiel chapters 40-48. It is as if Jesus Christ, the one who is efficacious, was not even present nor worth alluding to in the ineffectual literal fulfillment of the prophecies.

"The millennium could not be apart from the manifestation of Christ, upon whom the entire age depends."
"The millennium will be the period of the manifestation of the glory of the Lord Jesus Christ."
(Dwight Pentecost) *in His Book "THINGS TO COME" speaking of the Millennium Kingdom, page 478-480.*

<u>*This kind of emphasis on Jesus is nowhere to be found in Ezekiel 40-48, but rather the emphasis centers around the Temple and the Prince who sins.*</u>

<u>*Since Ezekiel 40-48 does not fit during the time of the Millennium, where would it fit?*</u>

(Keep in mind we only have a few options.)

(1.) The present time.
(2.) The Great Tribulation.
(3.) After the Great Tribulation and before the Millennium.
(4.) During the Millennium.
(5.) After the Millennium.

<u>*We should now be able to appreciate more why some people want to spiritualize Scripture or just flat do away with it.*</u>

(A careful examination reveals we are hard pressed to place Ezekiel 40-48 in any of the time frames mentioned above for a number of good reasons, some of which I have already mention within this book.)

One might ask, "What about now? Why <u>can't the temple be</u> <u>built now, and all these prophecies and promises of God be</u> <u>fulfilled now, before the Great Tribulation?</u>

The problem is we have a system in effect now, the New Covenant. The system revealed within Ezekiel 40-48 is a different system. It cannot be in effect with it's animal sacrificial Old Covenant system of atonement for sin, within the New Covenant.

Hebrews 8:13
When He said, "A new covenant," **He has made the first obsolete.** But whatever is becoming obsolete and growing old is ready to disappear.

Hebrews 7:26-27
For it was fitting for us to have such a high priest, holy, innocent, undefiled, separated from sinners and exalted above the heavens; 27) who does not need daily, like those high priests, to offer up sacrifices, first for His own sins and then for the sins of the people, **because this He did once for all when He offered up Himself.**

Considerations:

1. Does Ezekiel 38-39 run concurrently with 40-48?

A) If so where do they fit?

B) If not, then they represent two different time periods. Where would each fit?

2. The death of Jesus Christ is pivotal in moving out of the Old Covenant and into the New Covenant.

A) How can the obsolete system with it's animal sacrifice and other requirements (Ezekiel 40-48) be reenacted while the New Covenant is in effect or (while Jesus Christ is reigning on this earth, since Jesus died to put an end to it?) **Hebrews 9:16** *For where a covenant is, there must of necessity be the death of the one who made it.*

B) Would that obsolete system not undermine the **importance** of the sacrifice Jesus made when He died on the cross for man's sins and all that it accomplished and represents?

1 Corinthians 15:3-4
For I delivered to you as of **first importance** what I also received, that Christ died for our sins according to the Scriptures, 4) and that He was buried, and that He was raised on the third day according to the Scriptures,

Note: If Ezekiel 40-48 is placed in the Millennium a careful reading will indicates what is of first importance during the Millennium, and it's not Jesus Christ and all He did.

6

THE OPTION

What I am going to do in this chapter is to offer an option for you to consider without spiritualizing or doing away with Ezekiel 38-48. I am simply inserting a time period between the Rapture of the Body of Christ and the Great Tribulation. I believe this is a way in which you can have harmony with the Scriptures and have far fewer problems than any of the other positions.

My position does have some problems, which I will address; but again, I believe this approach has far less serious problems than any of the other views.

In helping to understand my view, I will start by asking a few questions.

Before Jesus was born, did the nation of Israel have all the information necessary to recognize Jesus as their Messiah?

As a result of the many miracles Jesus performed during His earthly ministry, did that enhance the nation of Israel's ability to recognize Jesus as their Messiah? Did the majority of the nation of Israel accept Jesus as their Messiah?

Acts 4:8-10

Then Peter, filled with the Holy Spirit, said to them, **" Rulers and elders of the people,** 9) if we are on trial today for a benefit done to a sick man, as to how this man has been made well, 10) let it be known to all of you and to all the people of Israel, that by the name of Jesus Christ the Nazarene, **whom you crucified,** whom God raised from the dead — by this name this man stands here before you in good health.

1 Thessalonians 2:14-15

For ye, brethren, became followers of the churches of God which in Judaea are in Christ Jesus: for ye also have suffered like things of your own countrymen, even as they have **of the Jews: 15) Who both killed the Lord Jesus,** and their own prophets, and have persecuted us; and they please not God, and are contrary to all men:

Do you think, as a result of the way the people of Israel treated their Messiah, Jesus Christ, that God stopped loving and caring for them?

Deuteronomy 7:1

"For you are a holy people to the LORD your God; the LORD your God has chosen you to be a people for His own possession out of all the peoples who are on the face of the earth.

QUESTION:

Since the time of the crucifixion of Jesus Christ, do you think the spiritual perception of the nation of Israel has increased or decreased?

Many in our day would say, for the most part, that many Jews are Jews in name only and do not represent what God had intended. They would support their view by claiming that most Jews today are liberal and secular, and care little about following the 613 laws.

Do you think that God's intent for the Jewish people has changed? Do you think God would like to see the Jewish people accept their Jewish Messiah?

Of course, we should all know that many of Jesus' followers were Jewish and the whole Body of Christ was Jewish to start with, for many years. But they were few in number compared to the nation of Israel.

Many contend that God's intent is to fulfill the Old Testament prophecy made to Israel, and for Israel to come to know their Messiah. How can that be accomplished?

Of course, God can do anything He desires any way He desires.
Note:
One essential way God has operated in the past is through the cooperative responses by His people.
This is a very important principle to understand.

Therefore, Israel would be expected to choose to believe in the Lord Jesus Christ as their Messiah and Savior. <u>How could that be possible in the day and age we live in? That is the question.</u> *Salvation has always been available for Israel on an individual basis, as it has been for everyone else. But how can you get the nation of Israel to turn around in this day and age, and trust in their Messiah, the Lord Jesus Christ?*

One of the main obstacles standing in Israel's way is the Church. Israelis strongly do not believe that the Christian Church represents their God.

How can that objection be dealt with and bring Israel to know and believe in their Messiah, the Lord Jesus Christ?

There you have it.

Out of God's love for His people and the truthfulness of His words, He will remove the Church. That includes the whole New Covenant system; so that prophecies can be fulfilled and another opportunity be given to Israel to know and believe in their Messiah - Jesus Christ, as some did while He was on earth.

"God will complete the program for the church before resuming His program with Israel."
(Dwight Pentecost) *in His Book "THINGS TO COME", page 410.*

What would the state of the world be like if all Christians were suddenly removed? 1 Corinthians 15:52 - 1 Thessalonians 4:17

There would be an economic collapse amongst other things, the result of world wide economical dependence.

<u>Question:</u>
Once the system of the Church is removed (The New Covenant) what would be left?

Answer:
The world would be like it was before the New Covenant was instituted, with the exception that God's people, the Jews, would be more spiritually dead than they were before Jesus Christ came and died for their sins. They would continue to hang onto the substance of their Judaism by a thumb nail.

Of course, that's not the desire of God for Israel; so therefore, we have Ezekiel 38-39.

As a result of the removing of the Church and then the inevitable world-wide economic collapse, the nations come together to attempt to solve their problems. There is peace, national survival is the issue. Nations form closer relationships than ever. Israel, although it's not effected as severely as other nations, simply because of the lack of Christians in key places within their government and economic system, join in the recovery process. Israel will prosper at a much faster rate than other nations, which causes resentment.

Before the removal of the Body Of Christ
Many nations have shown hatred towards Israel. The United States, with some of its key allies, have made it difficult for certain nations to do what they would like, which is eliminating Israel from the face of the earth.

Israel's population is about 1-1000th of the world's population; yet a lot of the tension within the world is tied directly or indirectly to Israel.

After the removal of the Body of Christ
There will be an inevitable economic collapse; much of the world's hatred toward Israel is set aside, merely because of the greater problem - their own survival.

After the Recovery

Once the sense of stability of the nations is restored, they once again start feeling their muscles. They are reminded of their hatred of Israel. Now the hatred is even more than ever, since Israel has blossomed during this worldwide economic disaster.

That's where Ezekiel 38-39 comes in.

Ezekiel 38:9

"You will go up, you will come like a storm; you will be like a cloud covering the land, you and all your troops, and many peoples with you."

Ezekiel 38:14-16

"Therefore prophesy, son of man, and say to Gog, 'Thus says the Lord GOD, "On that day when My people Israel are living securely, will you not know it? 15) "You will come from your place out of the remote parts of the north, you and many peoples with you, all of them riding on horses, a great assembly and a mighty army; 16) and you will come up against My people Israel like a cloud to cover the land. It shall come about in the last days that I will bring you against My land, so that the nations may know Me when I am sanctified through you before their eyes, O Gog."

Note: This event cannot be confused with Luke 21:20.
They are two different events.
In Ezekiel, Israel is rescued. In Luke, Israel suffers destruction.

Luke 21:20-21

"But when you see Jerusalem surrounded by armies, then recognize that her desolation is near.

Ezekiel 38-39 has to fit somewhere.

Where does it fit best?

It would make no sense to place it **during the seven year Tribulation** where you have, on the one hand, an army surrounding Israel and Israel being supernaturally rescued by God; and on the other hand, within a very short period of time, armies once again surrounding Israel for Israel's destruction. (Armageddon)

At the end of the Tribulation, Israel, for the most part, has been destroyed; so it certainly would not fit there.

The following verses refer to the end of the Tribulation period.
Isaiah 13:12
I will make mortal man scarcer than pure gold
And mankind than the gold of Ophir.

Isaiah 24:6
Therefore, a curse devours the earth, and those who live in it are held guilty. Therefore, the inhabitants of the earth are burned, and few men are left.

Matthew 24:22
"Unless those days had been cut short, no life would have been saved; but for the sake of the elect those days will be cut short.

Ezekiel 38-39 also would not fit during the Millennium. The whole atmosphere of the Millennium is not conducive to it. There will be no war during the Millennium.

Isaiah 65:25
"The wolf and the lamb will graze together, and the lion will eat straw like the ox; and dust will be the serpent's food. They will do no evil or harm in all My holy mountain," says the LORD."

Ezekiel 38-39 does not fit after the Millennium

I hardly think they are going to take time to bury the dead for 7 months and burn the weapons for seven years just prior to the Great White Throne Judgment.

It's interesting to consider where this judgment is going to take place. Rev. 20:11-12 says, "and I saw a great white throne and Him who sat on it, from whose presence earth and heaven fled away, and no place was found for them." Very interesting! The Great White Throne Judgment is not going to take place on earth or in the heavens as we know it. It is going to take place outside of the universe, and the earth and heavens are going to disappear. Rev. 21:1 says, "And I saw a new heaven and a new earth; for the first heaven and the first earth passed away, and there is no longer any sea."

So in the chronology of events, it is unreasonable to think people are going to take an addition 7 years to bury the dead and burn the weapons from the war of God and Magog at the end of the Millennium when the earth and heavens are going to immediately "flee away" and "pass away" (Rev. 20:11; 21:1), and a new heaven and earth are going to be created by God. It is much more reasonable to think that the 7 years of burying the dead and burning the weapons will take place some time other than at the end of the Millennium.

Plus, one of the main outcomes of Ezekiel 38-39 is that Israel and the nations would come to know that God is the God of Israel. But that is precisely what would have been going on for a thousand years during the Millennium. **Ezekiel 39:22** "And the house of Israel will know that I am the LORD their God from that day onward."

Revelation 20:9
And they came up on the broad plain of the earth and surrounded the camp of the saints and the beloved city, **and fire came down from heaven and devoured them.**
Note: In Ezekiel the armies come against Israel. There is no camp of the saints. Nor is the devil thrown into the lake of fire. In Ezekiel, Israel came out of exile, which would not have been the case during the Millennium in the book of Revelation.

**Keep in mind,** the result of God's intervention for Israel in Ezekiel 38-39.
Ezekiel 39:21
"And I will set My glory among the nations; and all the nations will see My judgment which I have executed and My hand which I have laid on them.

This prophecy would be a bit hard to fulfill if Ezekiel 38-39 were to be the same event as Revelation 20:9 simply because in Revelation 20:9 the nations are destroyed for the most part.

For a long time, Bible scholars have struggled to understand how the war of God and Magog in Ezekiel 38,39 fits with the war of God and Magog in Rev. 20, at the end of the Millennium, because so many of the details in Ezekiel just aren't reasonable, in real time, at the end of the Millennium.

A possible explanation of the Ezekiel war of God and Magog is that it has both "a near and far fulfillment." That is, there are two wars of Gog and Magog, one prior to the Tribulation, before the building of the Temple, and another one at the end of the Millennium, just before the Great White Throne Judgment.

A few men put the first war within the Tribulation, but as we've discussed, with all that is going on in the Tribulation period (Revelation 6-18), that seems unlikely. If we accept this explanation of the "near and far fulfillment", then there is application of the details in Ezekiel 38-39, in the first war of Gog and Magog and the second one (Rev 20).

As a result of the destruction of Gog and Magog in Ezekiel 39, God calls His people back to Israel. This would not be the case at the end of the Millennium, simply because they would have already been there.

Also in Ezekiel 39:22, as a result of God's intervention, the house of Israel will come to know their God. That does not seem to fit the end of the Millennium, simply because Israel would have just spent 1000 years with their God.

Now getting back to the story.

After the Recovery
Once the sense of stability of the nations is restored, they once again start feeling their muscles. They are reminded of their hatred of Israel. Now the hatred is even stronger than ever, since Israel has blossomed during this world wide economical disaster, due to resources.

That's where we pick up Ezekiel 38-39. This scenario occurs from the removal of the Church to renewed hatred for Israel.

Ezekiel 38:9

"You will go up, you will come like a storm; you will be like a cloud covering the land, you and all your troops, and many peoples with you."

The nations recover from the economic disaster and rekindle their hatred for Israel.

The question is: what do they do and how do they do it?

Many nations want to destroy Israel; but they do not want to be destroyed in the process. That would be inevitable if they were to approach the destruction of Israel in the normal conventional warfare mode, simply because Israel is highly armed and has nuclear weapons.

The idea:

Someone comes up with the idea of synchronizing their attack on Israel, so that many nations move on Israel at the same time. This would be just to Israel's borders. Not one shot is to be fired and not one person crosses the border into Israel.

They just surround Israel and in the following days continue to build an insurmountable force against Israel.

The question is: What does Israel do?

No one has fired a shot at Israel nor entered their country. All Israel sees is a massive army that has surrounded their country.

What can Israel do?

Keep in mind, there is no United States, as we know it today, to come to Israel's aid, since the Church has been removed (1 Corinthians 15:52 - 1 Thessalonians 4:17). This results in the United States becoming a limited-player within the nations.

What can Israel do?

The answer is, nothing.

They will not nuke the armies because in doing so they would nuke themselves. Israel is a small country.

Ezekiel 38:9

"You will go up, you will come like a storm; you will be like a cloud covering the land, you and all your troops, and many peoples with you."

Get the picture: All the world news stations will be covering this event. Everyone will be watching and waiting to see what happens to Israel.

Everyone on earth, including all Israelis, will be 100% convinced that once the armies start moving into Israel, there will be no more Jews.

Then on a given day, in a given hour, the armies will start crossing the borders and marching into Israel.

And Then:

Ezekiel 38:18-23

"It will come about on that day, when Gog comes against the land of Israel," declares the Lord GOD, "that My fury will mount up in My anger. 19) "In My zeal and in My blazing wrath I declare that on that day there will surely be a great earthquake in the land of Israel. 20) " The fish of the sea, the birds of the heavens, the beasts of the field, all the creeping things that creep on the earth, and all the men who are on the face of the earth will shake at My presence; the mountains also will be thrown down, the steep pathways will collapse and every wall will fall to the ground. 21) "I will call for a sword against him on all My mountains," declares the Lord GOD. " Every man's sword will be against his brother. 22) "With pestilence and with blood I will enter into judgment with him; and I will rain on him and on his troops, and on the many peoples who are with him, a torrential rain, with hailstones, fire and brimstone. 23) "I will magnify Myself, sanctify Myself, and make Myself known in the sight of many nations; and they will know that I am the LORD."

Ezekiel 39:3-6

"I will strike your bow from your left hand and dash down your arrows from your right hand. 4) "You will fall on the mountains of Israel, you and all your troops and the peoples who are with you; I will give you as food to every kind of predatory bird and beast of the field. 5) "You will fall on the open field; for it is I who have spoken," declares the Lord GOD. 6) "And I will send fire upon Magog and those who inhabit the coastlands in safety; and they will know that I am the LORD."

Ezekiel 38:18-23
Is a description of a visible, astonishing event that starts an incredible series of supernatural events on earth right up till and beyond the second coming of Jesus Christ.

As a result of this event, Israel and the people of the world will have an awareness of God that becomes obvious to all.

Ezekiel 39:21-22
"And I will set My glory among the nations; and all the nations will see My judgment which I have executed and My hand which I have laid on them. 22) "And the house of Israel will know that I am the LORD their God from that day onward."

Turn Around

Israel will have almost a complete turn around from liberal apathy towards God and his 613 laws to a resurgence of dedication that will be unmatched within the history of Israel. **Note:** this is not the return of the Holy Spirit that was "taken out of the way" with those He dwells in (2 Thessalonians 2:7 - 1 Thessalonians 4:17). Nor is it a resuming of the Body of Christ (the Church), rather a profound realization of their God.

The dedication and commitment is so great that even the unthinkable occurs.
(Which we would think of as child abuse, but they process it differently Deuteronomy 13:6-9).

Zechariah 13:3
"And if anyone still prophesies, then his father and mother who gave birth to him will say to him, 'You shall not live, for you have spoken falsely in the name of the LORD'; and his father and mother who gave birth to him will pierce him through when he prophesies.

Jews return to Israel from all the nations.

Ezekiel 39:26
"They will forget their disgrace and all their treachery which they perpetrated against Me, when they live securely on their own land with no one to make them afraid.

Ezekiel 39:28-29
"Then they will know that I am the LORD their God because I made them go into exile among the nations, and then gathered them again to their own land; and I will leave none of them there any longer. 29) "I will not hide My face from them any longer, for I will have poured out My Spirit on the house of Israel," declares the Lord GOD.

The chronology of the option is this:
1. The Body of Christ is removed, 1 Corinthians 15:52.
2. Ezekiel 38-39 occurs.
3. Then things move right into Ezekiel 40-48: the construction of the Ezekiel Temple as a result of a resurgence of dedication.
4. Time then moves right into the book of Revelation and to the Second coming of Christ, with the Millennium following.

Israel's resurgence of dedication to God provides a way of the fulfillment of Revelation 14:1-5 to occur.

Revelation 14:1-5
Then I looked, and behold, the Lamb was standing on Mount Zion, and with Him one hundred and forty-four thousand, having His name and the name of His Father written on their foreheads. 2) And I heard a voice from heaven, like the sound of many waters and like the sound of loud thunder, and the voice which I heard was like the sound of harpists playing on

their harps. 3) And they sang a new song before the throne and before the four living creatures and the elders; and no one could learn the song except the **one hundred and forty-four thousand** who had been purchased from the earth. 4) These are the ones who have not been defiled with women, for they have kept themselves chaste. These are the ones who follow the Lamb wherever He goes. These have been purchased from among men as first fruits to God and to the Lamb. 5) **And no lie was found in their mouth; they are blameless.**

Who today:
Is naive enough to think in our day we have 144,000 Jews, 12 thousand from each tribe that are blameless with no lie found in their mouth?

This is made possible by the rededication of Israel as a result of God rescuing them from annihilation, Ezekiel 38-39.

We all need to keep in mind
that Israel is the apple of God's eye.

Zechariah 2:8
For thus says the LORD of hosts, "After glory He has sent me against the nations which plunder you, for he who touches you, touches the apple of His eye.

God's love, mercy, and patience is off the charts.
He is faithful to His promises and His people.

Psalms 86:15
But You, O Lord, are a God merciful and gracious, slow to anger and abundant in loving kindness and truth.

Micah 7:18
Who is a God like You, who pardons iniquity and passes over the rebellious act of the remnant of His possession? He does not retain His anger forever, because He delights in unchanging love.

Sad as it is,
The history of mankind is pitiful in many respects. In the Garden, man falls; after the Flood Noah gets drunk; after the parting of the Red Sea Israel builds the golden calf; after the Law the crucifixion of the Messiah; after Pentecost man still sins; after the rescue of Ezekiel 38-39, mankind follows the Antichrist; and after the Millennium mankind attempts to kill Jesus and the Saints, Revelation 20:8-9.

Nonetheless God is Gracious!

So the option I am presenting in this book continues with the construction of the Ezekiel Temple in Ezekiel 40-48, following Ezekiel 38-39.

It should be noted that God came to rescue Israel in Ezekiel 38-39; but it's not the same kind of coming as the Second Coming where He touches down on the earth.

It is more like the coming of 1 Corinthians 15:52 or the many Old Testament examples dealing with Israel.

During the construction of the Ezekiel Temple, God is pro-active but just not on the earth in the same way He will be at the Second Coming and the Millennium, where he is bodily present.

In Ezekiel, God's glory will fill the Temple, as it does in the Temple that is in heaven, Revelation 11:19 - 14:15.

It's not the intent of Ezekiel 38-48 for Israel to come to believe in a coming Messiah. Rather that they would come to believe in their Messiah who has already come - Jesus.

During the times of the Tribulation, 144,000 Jews will believe in their Messiah who has come, Jesus Christ. Revelation 7:3-8

They will be like the Jewish believers during Jesus' earthly ministry before the Holy Spirit was given. John 7:39

They will become evangelists during the Tribulation, converting many to the Jewish Messiah Jesus Christ, the one who died for their sins and arose from the dead.

Note: Likely the identity of the 12 tribes is reestablished by God as part of the renewal of dedication in Ezekiel 38-39.

Revelation Chapters 5-22,
Chapter 5: Vision.
Chapter 6: Seals.
Chapter 7: The 144,000 Jews.
Chapter 8: Seals, Trumpets.
Chapter 9: Trumpets.
Chapter 10: The little book.
Chapter 11: The two witnesses.
Chapter 12: War.
Chapter 13: The beast and his prophet.
Chapter 14: Various announcements.
Chapter 15: Judgments to come.
Chapter 16: The bowl judgments.

Chapter 17: Religious Babylon destroyed.
Chapter 18: Commercial Babylon destroyed.
Chapter 19: The second coming of Christ.
Chapter 20: The Millennium.
Chapter 21: New heavens and new earth, eternity.
Chapter 22: New Jerusalem.

Precise instructions are given to the building of the Ezekiel Temple, none of which could be possible if God had not changed the topography of Israel in Ezekiel 38:20.

Ezekiel 38:20
"The fish of the sea, the birds of the heavens, the beasts of the field, all the creeping things that creep on the earth, and all the men who are on the face of the earth will shake at My presence; the mountains also will be thrown down, the steep pathways will collapse and every wall will fall to the ground.

There will be a sizable river flowing from the Temple, with fruit trees and "their leaves for healing." These are effectual reminders of what God did in rescuing Israel from annihilation.

Ezekiel 47:1
Then he brought me back to the door of the house; and behold, water was flowing from under the threshold of the house toward the east, for the house faced east. And the water was flowing down from under, from the right side of the house, from south of the altar.

Ezekiel 47:8
Then he said to me, "These waters go out toward the eastern region and go down into the Arabah; then they go toward the sea, being made to flow into the sea, and the waters of the sea become fresh.

The river in Ezekiel is not to be confused with the two rivers in the Millennium.

Zechariah 14:8
And it will come about in that day that living waters will flow out of Jerusalem, half of them toward the eastern sea and the other half toward the western sea; it will be in summer as well as in winter.

(Other Considerations:)

The Prince
There is much speculation about who the prince of Ezekiel 40-48 is; some think it's David. Regardless of who it is, the conditions change to the point that the antichrist eventually stands in the Temple.

Note: If it is David, it would seem he has a spiritual body that can still sin. Ezekiel 45:22

Is there a connection between the prince and the antichrist?

Matthew 24:15
"Therefore when you see the ABOMINATION OF DESOLATION which was spoken of through Daniel the prophet, standing in the holy place (let the reader understand),

J. Dwight Pentecost
The abomination of desolation (Matt 24:15) is clearly stated by Daniel (9:27) to appear in the middle of the week and continue to the end of the period.
(Things to come pg. 279)

Daniel 9:27
"And he will make a firm covenant with the many for one week, but in the middle of the week he will put a stop to sacrifice and grain offering; and on the wing of abominations will come one who makes desolate, even until a complete destruction, one that is decreed, is poured out on the one who makes desolate."

We have the vision of the Temple and a prince in Ezekiel 40-48, which is a future prophecy of a Temple to come. The only future prophecy of a Temple to come is found in the times of the Tribulation.

2 Thessalonians 2:4
Who opposes and exalts himself above every so-called god or object of worship, so that he takes his seat in the temple of God, displaying himself as being God.

Ephesians 2:2
in which you formerly walked according to the course of this world, **according to the prince of the power of the air,** of the spirit that is now working in the sons of disobedience.

Robert L. Thomas: This individual "opposes and exalts himself over everything that is called God or is worshiped." His direct and determined opposition to the true God will be a leading feature of the continuing apostasy. It will be especially marked by removal of the symbolic articles from the Jerusalem temple. The man of lawlessness will occupy the holy precincts in order to accept and even demand worship that is due God alone. This evidently is a Jewish temple to be rebuilt in Jerusalem in the future. Dependence of these words on Daniel 9:26, 27; 11:31, 36, 37; 12:11 (cf. Matt 24:15; Mark 13:14) demands such a reference. There is no impressive evidence for understanding naon ("temple") in a nonliteral sense. (*The Expositor's Bible Commentary, Vol 11 p.g. 322*)

Ezekiel 45:16
"All the people of the land shall give to this offering for the prince in Israel."

So we have prophecies pointing to a coming Temple and prince. The Temple will be there in the times of the Great Tribulation.

__I'm suggesting the Temple is built before the seven year Tribulation starts as a result of Ezekiel 38-39.__

Some ask:

Since the atmosphere of Ezekiel 44-48 in regard to the "prince" seems to be positive, how can I justify implying the prince could be the antichrist?

In response I admit it appears to be a cordial relationship between the prince (antichrist) and God. I also recognize his place within Israel is not opposed by God. I do point out though that we do have many cases in the Bible of similar circumstances.

For example:

Genesis 3:4-5
The serpent said to the woman, "You surely will not die! 5) "For God knows that in the day you eat from it your eyes will be opened, and you will be like God, knowing good and evil."

1. Who put the serpent in the garden?
2. What was the relationship between the Adam, Eve, and the serpent before the fall?
3. What was atmosphere like?
4. Was it cordial?
(It probably was, because we don't see Adam and Eve shrinking back from the serpent in fear or disgust.)

In Heaven:

Revelation 12:7-9
And there was war in heaven, Michael and his angels waging war with the dragon. The dragon and his angels waged war, 8) and they were not strong enough, and there was no longer a place found for them in heaven. 9) And the great dragon was thrown down, **the serpent of old who is called the devil and Satan,** who deceives the whole world; he was thrown down to the earth, and his angels were thrown down with him.

Before the war in heaven, what was the atmosphere?
Was it cordial?

As strange as it may appear to us, satan has apparently had the freedom to come and go in and out of God's very presence whenever he pleased with no fear of restraint or attack.

Job 2:1
Again there was a day when the sons of God came to present themselves before the LORD, and Satan also came among them to present himself before the LORD.

On earth:

Keep in mind who is responsible for abortions, rapes, wars, heart ache and hatred, the deceiver.

Ephesians 2:1-2
And you were dead in your trespasses and sins, 2) in which you formerly walked according to the course of this world, according to the **prince of the power of the air,** of the spirit that is now working in the sons of disobedience.

John 8:44
"You are of your father the devil, and you want to do the desires of your father. He was a murderer from the beginning, and does not stand in the truth because there is no truth in him. Whenever he speaks a lie, he speaks from his own nature, for he is a liar and the father of lies.

In Heaven:

It is interesting to recognize that the devil enters into the presence of the Lord in heaven even right now.
I wonder what the atmosphere is like?
Is it cordial?
While maybe not "cordial" based on friendship, it is likely cordial based on the permission of God for him to be there.

Revelation 12:10
"Now the salvation, and the power, and the kingdom of our God and the authority of His Christ have come, **for the accuser of our brethren** has been thrown down, **he who accuses them before our God day and night.**

Luke 22:31
"Simon, Simon, behold, **Satan has demanded permission** to sift you like wheat;

Job 2:4-6
Satan answered the LORD and said, "Skin for skin! Yes, all that a man has he will give for his life. 5) " However, put forth Your hand now, and touch his bone and his flesh; he will curse You to Your face." 6) **So the LORD said to Satan,** "Behold, he is in your power, only spare his life."

So we can see this (pardon the expression) relationship between God and Satan has been going on for a very long time.

Job 1:9-12
Then Satan answered the LORD, "Does Job fear God for nothing? 10) " Have You not made a hedge about him and his house and all that he has, on every side? You have blessed the work of his hands, and his possessions have increased in the land. 11) " But put forth Your hand now and touch all that he has; he will surely curse You to Your face." 12) **Then the LORD said to Satan,** "Behold, all that he has is in your power, only do not put forth your hand on him." **So Satan departed from the presence of the LORD.**

So now, why is it hard for us to consider the possibility that the "prince" in Ezekiel, the "deceiver" attempts to come between Israel and God and finally displays himself in the Ezekiel Temple as the antiChrist?

Daniel 9:26
"Then after the sixty-two weeks the Messiah will be cut off and have nothing, and the people of the **prince who is to come** will destroy the city and the sanctuary. And its end will come with a flood; even to the end there will be war; desolations are determined.

In this verse, the antichrist is called "the prince who is to come." This verse refers both to the destruction of Jerusalem in 70 AD and also within the context of the next verse (vs. 27) the identity of the prince who is to come is without doubt the antichrist.

So the antichrist is actually called a prince, which makes it not so much of a stretch to say that the prince of Ezekiel 43-48, could be the antichrist.

_____

Ezekiel 44:9 'Thus says the Lord GOD, "No foreigner uncircumcised in heart and uncircumcised in flesh, of all the foreigners who are among the sons of Israel, shall enter My sanctuary.

So........how would the antichrist be allowed to enter this temple?

My response is:

The anti-christ is a false imitation of Christ who was a Jew. So what would prevent the antichrist from being a Jew or even part Jew?

Many people think that the antichrist will likely be a Jew, because we know that he will sign a covenant (a treaty) with Israel for seven years, guaranteeing their security. It is highly unlikely that Israel would place their security into the hands of anyone who was not a Jew.

The real question here is, since the full glory of God's presence is in this Ezekiel Temple according to chapter 43, how is it that He would allow the antichrist to come into His Temple and defile it with Him there? The answer to that is, He will probably withdraw from it because of sin, as He did with Solomon's Temple (see Ezekiel 10 and 11).

God is in control of all things, and if it is His will to allow His Temple to be desecrated as a part of His overall plan of exposing evil and redeeming a people for Himself, then yes, He will allow it. Many things in God's eternal plan seem very strange to us, and this is certainly one of those things.

But maybe that is one reason why He Himself will be the Temple in eternity, because there is an inherent danger in having a temple, a building, apart from Himself. It may be difficult for us to conceive of God Himself being a Temple, but when we get to heaven, many of these things will be completely understandable and rational. Where we have the difficulty is trying to conceive of heavenly things while we are still here on earth. But the whole realm of heaven is going to consist of things completely unlike the earth as we know it now.

So the possibility of the prince of Ezekiel 43-48 being the antichrist may not be as much of a stretch as we might think at first.

The question is asked:

In Ezekiel 43:7-9 God speaks of the Temple as where the soles of His feet will stand, where He will dwell among the sons of Israel forever.

I place the building of the Ezekiel Temple after the rapture and before the Tribulation starts, indicating the Ezekiel Temple is the Temple of the Tribulation times that the antichrist will defile. It's asked how can I reconcile this knowing what Ezekiel 43:7-9 is saying?

So the question is: If God is going to dwell in the Ezekiel Temple forever, how is it that He would allow the antichrist to come into it and defile it?

Ezekiel 43:7-9
He said to me, "Son of man, this is the place of My throne and the place of the soles of My feet, **where I will dwell among the sons of Israel forever.** And the house of Israel will not again defile My holy name, neither they nor their kings, by their harlotry and by the corpses of their kings when they die, 8) by setting their threshold by My threshold and their door post beside My door post, with only the wall between Me and them. And they have defiled My holy name by their abominations which they have committed. So I have consumed them in My anger. 9) "Now let them put away their harlotry and the corpses of their kings far from Me; **and I will dwell among them forever.**

I respond by pointing out that their interpretation of Ezekiel 43:7-9 is incorrect. They are indicating that it is the Ezekiel Temple where God will dwell among the sons of Israel forever, which is false.

How we know that is because of Revelation 21:22.

Revelation 21:22
I saw no temple in it, for the Lord God the Almighty and the Lamb are its temple.

In the new heaven and a new earth there is not going to be a physical temple like what was being described in the book of Ezekiel, so therefore, God is not going to dwell forever in the Ezekiel Temple.

I believe God was using the Ezekiel Temple as a type to illuminate the heavenly Temple (God) and communicate the assurance all spiritual Israel (Romans 2:28 - 9:6) should have in their relationship with Him. When everything related to time is finished, and we are all in heaven together in the new heaven and new earth. God Himself will be the Temple.

Revelation 21:1-3
Then I saw a new heaven and a new earth; for the first heaven and the first earth passed away, and there is no longer any sea. **2) And I saw the holy city, new Jerusalem, coming down out of heaven from God,** made ready as a bride adorned for her husband. 3) And I heard a loud voice from the throne, saying, **"Behold, the tabernacle of God is among men, and He will dwell among them,** and they shall be His people, and God Himself will be among them,

Revelation 21:12
It had a great and high wall, with twelve gates, and at the gates twelve angels; and names were written on them, **which are the names of the twelve tribes of the sons of Israel.**

We can conclude from Ezekiel 43:7-9 that God will dwell forever among the saints of all ages. It is not saying that He will live eternally in the Ezekiel Temple. His throne will be in the New Jerusalem, His people will be in the New Jerusalem, and He will dwell among them forever. This is exactly what Ezekiel 43:7-9 says. It does not say that He will dwell in the Ezekiel Temple forever.

What about the supernatural things in Ezekiel 38-48?

For example:
Ezekiel 47:8
Then he said to me, "These waters go out toward the eastern region and go down into the Arabah; then they go toward the sea, being made to flow into the sea, and the waters of the sea become fresh."

My answer is the same as to how I explain this event:

Revelation 8:8
And the second angel sounded, and something like a great mountain burning with fire was thrown into the sea; and a third of the sea became blood;

God's sovereignty has the right to use supernatural events as well as natural events to accomplish His purposes however and whenever He wants.

Important consideration:

The Millennium will be centered around the one sacrifice that was made by Jesus Christ for all times.

1 Corinthians 3:11
For no man can lay a foundation other than the one which is laid, which is Jesus Christ.

This is the very opposite of the foundation being laid within the Millennium if Ezekiel 40-48 is applied to the Millennium.

The Millennium

This is where the Lord Jesus Christ reigns in person. Abraham, Moses, Jacob, Isaiah, Jeremiah along with the Old Covenant prophets and the elect are all there; Peter, Paul, all the apostles, martyrs, and members of the Body of Christ are also present. They are all there and accessible to the mortal people of the Millennium.

**During the Millennium,** Satan and his demons are removed. All forms of evil will be destroyed. The holiness and the glory of God will be apparent to all. People will be living for hundreds of years. The wolf and the lamb will dwell together in peace.

With this picture

of holiness and peace dominating during the Millennium, it is inconceivable to me that we will still have a desire for wealth, laziness, fornication, immorality, jealousy, dissension, drunkenness, and pride. In addition, there will no longer be a desire for fame, doubts, unforgivingness, silly talk, hypocrisy, abortion, outbursts of anger, filthy language, worldliness, impatience, unkindness, apathy, obscene jokes, overeating, lust of the eyes, lust of the mind, lying, gossip, critical spirit, lack of self control, hate, getting even, disrespectfulness, unfaithfulness, stealing, worrying, backbiting, wrong attitudes, and idols.

All of the above are the result of a sinful nature. A sin nature, without exception, cannot help itself; it has to produce sin just as an apple tree produces apples. Therefore I believe that people during the Millennium will not have a sin nature.

Man can sin without a sinful nature, as evidenced by Adam and Eve. The difference is that before the fall, they had a choice to sin or not to sin. After the fall, everyone has to sin because of their nature. A bad root produces bad fruit.

I am not saying that sin will not occur during the Millennium. All I am saying is that sin will be the exception, not the rule, as a sinful nature requires. This is evident within our time period with members of the Body of Christ being indwelt with the Holy Spirit (God), still sinning: the result of having two natures within.

I am not saying a Christian cannot go for a season without sinning, but what I am saying is that the old ugly head of sin will always surface in everyone. This is incompatible with the period of the Millennium.

<u>That's why with all the sinning going on in Ezekiel 40-48, Ezekiel 40-48 does not fit the picture of the Millennium being a holy time and place. You can't have it both ways.</u>

Note: what would be the purpose of replaying the same old drama within the time of the Millennium? It's been played out every way imaginable for thousands and thousands of years.

The Millennium represents a new way that God will be dealing with the human race. It's similar to the Garden of Eden, with the exception that the numbers are far greater in comparison, setting forth eternal principles.

<u>After the Millennium</u> is the final effort to get rid of God, revealing mankind's heart independent of God, just before the Great White Throne Judgment.

Man and Lucifer (Satan) were created to be dependent upon God just as those living during the Millennium will be.

<u>When dependence is exchanged for desires of independence, overt sin is waiting at the door. All living during the Millennium know the truth, yet shortly after the Millennium the glorious relationship with God is exchanged for independence resulting in rebellion just like Satan.</u>

The people of the Millennium are not saved as we are and indwelt with the Holy Spirit. One of the many reasons is because they end up attempting to destroy and kill the Lord Jesus Christ.

I do not believe people indwelt with the Holy Spirit (GOD) could do such a thing. (It's the Holy Spirit). I look at the people of the Millennium as similar to Adam who, originally had no sin nature, but who knowingly chose to sin.

Note: Not all the angels fell. Therefore, some people during the Millennium surely will be saved. They are the ones who believe correctly and worship correctly the Lord Jesus Christ.

A sin nature would contaminate the Millennium.

One main difference between the garden situation before the fall and the parallel garden situation during the Millennium is that there is no tree in the Millennium garden until after the Millennium is over. There is not much to tempt people to use their free will to do anything but what is right and good, until Satan the deceiver is loosed.

Right after

the 1000 year Millennium, events do not progress immediately to the Great White Throne Judgment. There is a time period between the two events required for Satan to deceive the nations, gather the armies in order to make war against the camp of the saints, the beloved city, and the Lord Jesus Christ. **Revelation 20:7-9**

The Great White Throne Judgment

Revelation 20:11-15

Then I saw a great white throne and Him who sat upon it, from whose presence earth and heaven fled away, and no place was found for them. 12) And I saw the dead, the great and the small, standing before the throne, and books were opened; and another book was opened, which is the book of life; and the dead were judged from the things which were written in the books, according to their deeds. 13) And the sea gave up the dead which were in it, and death and Hades gave up the dead which were in them; and they were judged, every one of them according to their deeds. 14) Then death and Hades were thrown into the lake of fire. This is the second death, the lake of fire. 15) And if anyone's name was not found written in the book of life, he was thrown into the lake of fire.

Keep in mind that this Judgment is not so that God can find out anything He did not already know, nor will it will change anything that has already been determined. It's simply for the benefit of those in the Books to know for certain why they will spend eternity in the Lake of Fire. This judgment will reveal mankind's prideful, rebellious, sinful nature and God's grace, rightness, and justice.

The New Heaven and a New Earth

Revelation 21:12-14
It had a great and high wall, with twelve gates, and at the gates twelve angels; and names were written on them, which are those of the **twelve tribes** of the sons of Israel. 13) There were three gates on the east and three gates on the north and three gates on the south and three gates on the west. 14) And the wall of the city had twelve foundation stones, and on them were the twelve names of the **twelve apostles** of the Lamb.

The identity of Israel and the Body of Christ as being two separate groups continues into the New Heaven and Earth. (Revelation 21: 12-14)

Isaiah 66:22 "For just as the new heavens and the new earth which I make will endure before Me," declares the LORD, "So your offspring and your name will endure."

(Isaiah 66:22 is an Old Testament prophecy being fulfilled in the New Heaven and Earth.)

Isaiah 65:17-18
For behold, I create new heavens and a new earth; and the former things shall not be remembered or come to mind. 18) But be glad and rejoice forever in what I create; for behold, I create Jerusalem for rejoicing, and her people for gladness.

Revelation 21:22-27
I saw no temple in it, for the Lord God the Almighty and the Lamb are its temple. 23) And the city has no need of the sun or of the moon to shine on it, for the glory of God has illumined it, and its lamp is the Lamb. 24) The nations will walk by its light, and the kings of the earth will bring their glory into it. 25) In the daytime (for there will be no night there) its gates will never be closed; 26) and they will bring the glory and the honor of the nations into it; 27) and nothing unclean, and no one who practices abomination and lying, shall ever come into it, but only those whose names are written in the Lamb's book of life.

Revelation 22:14-15
Blessed are those who wash their robes, that they may have the right to the tree of life, and may enter by the gates into the city. 15) Outside are the dogs and the sorcerers and the immoral persons and the murderers and the idolaters, and everyone who loves and practices lying.

Revelation 22:20
He who testifies to these things says, "Yes, I am coming quickly." Amen. Come, Lord Jesus.

Summary:

Ezekiel 38-48 does not fit within:

1. <u>The present time.</u>
A) Covenant conflict.

2. <u>The Great Tribulation.</u>
A) Israel is rescued in Ezekiel.
Nearly destroyed in the Tribulation.

3. <u>After the Great Tribulation and before the Millennium.</u>
A.) The armies have already been destroyed at Armageddon.
There are no goats left Matt 25:41.

4. <u>During the Millennium.</u>
A) No war in the Millennium.
B) Inefficacious fulfillment of literal prophecy to Israel is not believable. Plus Jesus is the effectual one time sacrifice.

5. <u>After the Millennium.</u>
A) Does not fit, Israel already knows God, as a result of the 1000 year Millennium.

Now for a recap.

1. Rapture: 1 Corinthians 15:52

Before the rapture, there will be wars and rumors of wars (Matthew 24:6-8. It will be like the days of Noah (Luke 17:26-27). No one will know the hour of His coming (Matthew 24:44). There will be no signs to be observed before the Rapture (Luke 17:20). Just as the lightning flashes, so it will be at His coming (Luke 17:24). All believers will be caught up in the clouds to meet the Lord (1 Thessalonians 4:17).

2. Gog Magog: Ezekiel 38-39

After the Rapture, there will likely be a massive worldwide crisis over the disappearance of so many people. A global government may emerge. Israel will find itself in a time of peace and safety (Ezekiel 38:8-11) and will become very prosperous. In time, hatred for the Jews resurfaces and an alliance of nations will come against Israel (Ezekiel 38:9-16). God will supernaturally destroy the armies and rearrange the topography of the land of Israel (Ezekiel 38:18-21). This becomes a testimony to the world that the God of Israel reigns (Ezekiel 39:7-21): Many Jews will experience a rededication to God (Ezekiel 29:22-27-28).

3. Ezekiel Temple: Ezekiel 40-48

Shortly after Israel's rededication to God, they will start to build the Temple of God as outlined in Ezekiel 40-43. There is a return to the system that was in effect prior to the New Covenant, with blood atonement burnt offerings and sin offerings (Ezekiel 43:18-27). The uncircumcised will not be permitted to enter the Temple (Ezekiel 44:9). All of the requirements for the Temple are outlined in Ezekiel 40-48. I believe this is the same Temple spoken of in Matthew 24:15 and 2 Thessalonians 2:4; so therefore, the Ezekiel Temple moves right into the times of the Great Tribulation and the book of Revelation.

4. Tribulation 70th week: Revelation 6-18

Many Jews start becoming aware that the one they crucified, Jesus, was their Messiah. Their eyes are opened and 144,000 are saved and become witnesses for their Messiah, the Lord Jesus Christ (Revelation 7:4-8, Ezekiel 29:29). But many other Jews will follow the antichrist, who is referred to as "the Prince" (Daniel 9:26, 2 Thessalonians 2:4). The Judgments of God and acts of the antichrist are seen in Revelation 6-18.

The antichrist will be the supreme ruler over a global government and will require everyone to worship him.

5. <u>Second Coming: Revelation 19</u>

At Jesus' 2nd coming, He will fight and win the Battle of Armageddon, cast the Antichrist and false prophet into the lake of fire, and will separate the sheep from the goats (Matthew 25:31-46). Jesus' second coming is exactly 1260 days from the appearance of the Abomination of Desolation standing in the holy place (Matthew 24:15). Signs of Jesus Christ's return appear in the sky, the sun will be darkened and the moon will not give light (Matthew 24:39). All the people around the world will see Jesus returning (Matthew 24:30) (Acts 1:11).

6. <u>Millennium Revelation 20</u>

The sheep will go into the Millennium. Satan will be bound for a thousand years (Revelation 20:1-4).
Jesus Christ will reign over the earth and we will reign with Him. At the end of the thousand years, Satan will be released and will deceive the nations into making war against Jesus Christ one last time, unsuccessfully (Revelation 20:7-9). The last event before eternity is the Great White Throne Judgment (Revelation 20:11-15).

7. Eternity Revelation 21-22

Eternity will begin with the New Heaven, New Earth and the New Jerusalem where the Lord God the Almighty and the Lamb are its temple. Everything in the previous ages will pass away: sin, death, mourning, etc. The New Jerusalem is described in detail: it will be the awesome dwelling place of God Himself, and we will be able to go in and out of it. There will be no need of a sun or moon or night. We will see God's face, serve Him and reign with Him forever.

THE END

THE NEW BEGINNING

TRUST JESUS

TODAY!

APPENDIX

The Way of Salvation

Genesis 1:1
In the beginning God created the heavens and the earth.

Genesis 1:27
And God created man in His own image, in the image of God He created him; male and female He created them.

Genesis 1:31
And God saw all that He had made, and behold, **it was very good.** And there was evening and there was morning, the sixth day.

Genesis 2:16-17
And the LORD God commanded the man, saying, "From any tree of the garden you may eat freely; 17) but from the tree of the knowledge of good and evil you shall not eat, for in the day that you eat from it you shall surely die."

Genesis 3:6
When the woman saw that the tree was good for food, and that it was a delight to the eyes, and that the tree was desirable to make one wise, she took from its fruit and ate; and she gave also to her husband with her, and he ate.

It is important to keep in mind that God did not need to create mankind for any reason. He was totally complete within His own existence.

Genesis 1:26
Then God said, "Let Us make man in Our image, according to Our likeness; and let them rule over the fish of the sea and over the birds of the sky and over the cattle and over all the earth, and over every creeping thing that creeps on the earth."

It is also important to keep in mind that all that God created was good. God created man to love Him, not because man had to, but because man would desire to. Therefore, God provided a way for man to freely choose; he could love God or he could turn his back on Him and do his own thing in opposition to God's original desire in creating man. The true value of a love relationship is when one has the ability not to love yet still does. But love, by definition, must be freely given, not coerced. God does not grab us by the neck and order us to love Him. That would not be love.

When Adam and Eve, according to Genesis, ate the fruit God had commanded them not to eat, that act demonstrated man's desire to do his own thing and dissipated his love relationship with God, which was really rebellion against God. Even though it sounds like just eating a piece of fruit doesn't sound so bad, it was what that showed about the human heart that was bad; so consequently it introduced sin into the human race. Sin is what happens when we separate ourselves from God and do our own thing.

The result was separation from God; we became a substandard creation and our relationship with God was broken. Instead of being united with God in continual fellowship, which is what we were created to be, we became different from Him in form and substance. Oil does not mix with water and sin does not mix with God's holiness. We became legally separated from God and spiritually dead. God hates sin because He is pure and holy.

Isaiah 6:3

And one called out to another and said, "Holy, Holy, Holy, is the LORD of hosts, the whole earth is full of His glory."

As a result of the substandard creation that came into existence many things changed as a result of mans free choice to sin.

We now have wars, crime, death, pollution, divorce, sickness, lawlessness, birth defects, greed, hatred, insanity, earthquakes, riots, etc. It was neither God's intention nor fault but it was and is the penalty that God placed on us for our rebellion and sin but God still desired to have a love relationship with us.

God certainly knew what was to happen from the beginning of His creation, but knowing and controlling are two different things. One might ask the question, "If God knew in advance that man would sin, why did He create man?" I believe the answer to that question comes at the end of the story not at the beginning. The eternal value of the love relationship far exceeds the pitfalls of the rebellion.

Romans 11:33-34

Oh, the depth of the riches both of the wisdom and knowledge of God! How unsearchable are His judgments and unfathomable His ways! 34) For who has known the mind of the Lord, or who became His counselor?

So the seed of sin was imbedded within Adam and passed to all his offspring. Horses bare horses, fish bare fish, birds bare birds and sinful men bare sinful men.

Romans 5:12
Therefore, just as through one man sin entered into the world, and death through sin, and so death spread to all men, because all sinned...

The good news is that God provides a way of redemption and salvation. He provides a way of escape out of our sinful state.

Genesis 22:18
"And in your seed (God said to Abraham), all of the nations of the earth shall be blessed, because you have obeyed My voice."

God gave Abraham a faith test and he passed the test, resulting in God's promise that He would provide a descendent (Christ) who would reverse the damage that sin had done. God Himself would provide a way for our sins to be forgiven through a very unusual plan. The Bible says that before the foundation of the world, God decreed that His own Son would become a man, die on the cross and shed His blood so that sin's penalty would be paid. This is often hard for us to understand.

It wouldn't have been the plan that we would have come up with but God had to plan something that would satisfy His justice. He couldn't just forget about sin or get rid of it with a swipe of His hand. In His wisdom He knew that blood had to be shed because life is in the blood. Since sin requires death (separation), the taking of life (relationship) was the only way that sin could be paid for.

So God decided that His own beloved Son would give His life for our sin and become our Savior. But how could God convince man that he needed a Savior? In order for people to appreciate redemption (a Savior}, they first have to come to the realization they need one. So God gave Abraham's descendants the Law to be a testimony to the nations, showing God's righteousness and demonstrating man's sinfulness. This was to be a temporary system until all was fulfilled and Christ provided redemption for man's rebellion.

Galatians 3:16-19

Now the promises were spoken to Abraham and to his seed. He does not say, "And to seeds," as referring to many, but rather to one, "And to your seed," that is, Christ. 17) What I am saying is this: the Law, which came four hundred and thirty years later, does not invalidate a covenant previously ratified by God, so as to nullify the promise. 18) For if the inheritance is based on law, it is no longer based on a promise; but God has granted it to Abraham by means of a promise. 19) Why the Law then? It was added because of transgressions, having been ordained through angels by the agency of a mediator, **until** the seed should come to whom the promise had been made.

Galatians 2:21

I do not nullify the grace of God; for if righteousness comes through the Law, then Christ died needlessly.

This wonderful truth should be enough for all of us to leap for joy! If it were not for Abraham's seed (Jesus Christ) paying the penalty our sinful nature deserved, we would have no hope.

1 Corinthians 15:20-22

But now Christ has been raised from the dead, the first fruits of those who are asleep. 21) For since by a man came death, by a man also came the resurrection of the dead. 22) For as in Adam all die, so also in Christ all shall be made alive.

John 14:6
Jesus said to him, "I am the way, and the truth, and the life; no one comes to the Father, but through Me."

Every person alive can be saved if they will trust in Jesus Christ, the only provision God has made for their redemption. Keep in mind there was only one tree in the garden they were not to eat from; so also now there is only one way of undoing what was done. The eating of the fruit was a very easy and simple thing to do and it changed the course of the world. Trusting in Jesus is easier and simpler than the eating of the fruit. Trusting in Jesus will change the course of your life for all eternity. The eating of the fruit required a rebellious heart. Trusting in Jesus requires a humble heart.

2 Peter 3:9
The Lord is not slow about His promise, as some count slowness, but is patient toward you, not wishing for any to perish but for all to come to repentance.

John 1:9-13
There was the true light which, coming into the world, enlightens every man. 10) He was in the world, and the world was made through Him, and the world did not know Him. 11) He came to His own, and those who were His own did not receive Him. 12) But as many as received Him, to them He gave the right to become children of God, even to those who believe in His name, 13)who were born not of blood, nor of the will of the flesh, nor of the will of man, but of God.

John 1:17
For the Law was given through Moses; grace and truth were realized through Jesus Christ.

John 3:3-6-7
Jesus answered and said to him, "Truly, truly, I say to you, unless one is born again, he cannot see the kingdom of God." 6) "That which is born of the flesh is flesh, and that which is born of the Spirit is spirit. 7) "Do not marvel that I said to you, 'You must be born again.'"

John 4:13-14
Jesus answered and said to her, "Everyone who drinks of this water shall thirst again; but whoever drinks of the water that I shall give him shall never thirst; 14) but the water that I shall give him shall become in him a well of water springing up to eternal life."

Ephesians 2:8-9
For by grace you have been saved through faith; and that not of yourselves, it is the gift of God; 9) not as a result of works, that no one should boast.

John 5:24
"Truly, truly, I say to you, he who hears My word, and believes Him who sent Me, has eternal life, and does not come into judgment, but has passed out of death into life."

1 Peter 1:3-9
Blessed be the God and Father of our Lord Jesus Christ, who according to His great mercy has caused us to be born again to a living hope through the resurrection of Jesus Christ from the dead, 4) to obtain an inheritance which is imperishable and undefiled and will not fade away, reserved in heaven for you,

5) who are protected by the power of God through faith for a salvation ready to be revealed in the last time. 6) In this you greatly rejoice, even though now for a little while, if necessary, you have been distressed by various trials, 7) that the proof of your faith, being more precious than gold which is perishable, even though tested by fire, may be found to result in praise and glory and honor at the revelation of Jesus Christ; 8) and though you have not seen Him, you love Him, and though you do not see Him now, but believe in Him, you greatly rejoice with joy inexpressible and full of glory, 9) obtaining as the outcome of your faith the salvation of your souls.

Trusting in Jesus, or salvation, is as easy as lifting your heart to God and telling Him in your own words that you are tired of living a sinful life and you want Him to save you. You don't have to worry about cleaning your life up first because that is impossible to do anyway. The only way to get a clean life is for Jesus to forgive you. No matter what you have done, God invites you to come to Him and be saved because no matter how bad you think you are, God's love and grace are always greater than your sin.

You can never out-sin God's ability to forgive. When Jesus forgives and saves you, His Spirit comes into your life and enables you to be clean and to start changing.

The Bible says that when you are saved, you become a new creature, a new creation, just the reverse of what happened to Adam. You become a different person than you were before. You have different desires - you will want to read and study the Bible and learn about God. You will want to please Him. He will help you get rid of sinful habits - sometimes this happens immediately, sometimes it takes awhile. But you will change and it will pleasantly surprise you.

You will become a member of God's family. Many of us don't have much of a family here, but belonging to God's family is a wonderful privilege. When you are saved, it is important for you to get to know other Christians and go to a Bible-believing church so that you can grow in your faith. You will want to start sharing your faith and tell others what God has done for you. This is the most exciting adventure you will ever start on. It is awesome!

If you have read to the end of this Book and know that you have never become a Christian, but would like to, or if you would just like to know more about it, please feel free to call the number below. I would consider it a privilege to talk with you, answer your questions, and help you get to know God. Just go for it -Trust Jesus.

Romans 10:9-10
If you confess with your mouth Jesus as Lord, and believe in your heart that God raised Him from the dead, you shall be saved; 10) for with the heart man believes, resulting in righteousness, and with the mouth he confesses, resulting in salvation.

Acts 16:30-31
And after he brought them out, he said, "Sirs, what must I do to be saved?" 31) And they said, "Believe in the Lord Jesus, and you shall be saved, you and your household."

Feel free to contact me:
James Webber
503-816-5842
jwww@earthlink.net

"As I see it, the object of life is to find out what pleases God, and then just keep doing it."--Jim

If we can be of service to you, your group, or church, let us know. We are available for conferences, concerts, or seminars.

Please contact us Jim and Toni Webber at 503-816-5842 or email: jwww@earthlink.net.

For additional copies of James Webber's books:
Word Power, Study Power, Blood Power, End Times Power, Bible Power and Philosophy Power:

Go to: http://www.amazon.com/
In the search box, type in, the title by James Webber,
For example: End Times Power by James Webber

14489852R00076

Made in the USA
Charleston, SC
14 September 2012